The Civil War

by Timothy Levi Biel

America's WARS

Lucent Books, P.O. Box 289011, San Diego, CA 92198-9011

Books in the America's Wars Series:

The Revolutionary War
The Indian Wars
The War of 1812
The Mexican-American War
The Civil War
The Spanish-American War

World War I
World War II: The War in the Pacific
World War II: The War in Europe
The Korean War
The Vietnam War
The Persian Gulf War

Library of Congress Cataloging-in-Publication Data

Biel, Timothy L.
   The Civil War / by Timothy Levi Biel.
        p.   cm. — (America's wars)
   Includes bibliographical references and index.
   Summary: Examines the political, cultural, and military aspects of
the conflict that tragically divided the United States in the mid-
nineteenth century.
   ISBN 1-56006-404-8
   1. United States—History—Civil War, 1861-1865—Juvenile
literature.   [1. United States—History—Civil War, 1861-1865.]
   I. Title.   II. Series.
   E468.B54   1991
   973.7—dc20   91-29500
                                                       CIP
                                                       AC

Printed in the USA

Contents

Foreword

War, justifiable or not, is a descent into madness. George Washington, America's first president and commander-in-chief of its armed forces, wrote that his most fervent wish was "to see this plague of mankind, war, banished from the earth." Most, if not all of the forty presidents who succeeded Washington have echoed similar sentiments. Despite this, not one generation of Americans since the founding of the republic has been spared the maelstrom of war. In its brief history of just over two hundred years, the United States has been a combatant in eleven major wars. And four of those conflicts have occurred in the last fifty years.

America's reasons for going to war have differed little from those of most nations. Political, social, and economic forces were at work which either singly or in combination ushered America into each of its wars. A desire for independence motivated the Revolutionary War. The fear of annihilation led to the War of 1812. A related fear, that of having the nation divided, precipitated the Civil War. The need to contain an aggressor nation brought the United States into the Korean War. And territorial ambition lay behind the Mexican-American and the Indian Wars. Like all countries, America, at different times in its history, has been victimized by these forces and its citizens have been called to arms.

Whatever reasons may have been given to justify the use of military force, not all of America's wars have been popular. From the Revolutionary War to the Vietnam War, support of the people has alternately waxed and waned. For example, less than half of the colonists backed America's war of independence. In fact, most historians agree that at least one-third were committed to maintaining America's colonial status. During the Spanish-American War, a strong antiwar movement also developed. Resistance to the war was so high that the Democratic party made condemning the war a significant part of its platform in an attempt to lure voters into voting Democratic. The platform stated that "the burning issue of imperialism growing out of the Spanish war involves the very existence of the Republic and the destruction of our free institutions." More recently, the Vietnam War divided the nation like no other conflict had since the Civil War. The mushrooming antiwar movements in most major cities and colleges throughout the United States did more to bring that war to a conclusion than did actions on the battlefield.

Yet, there have been wars which have enjoyed overwhelming public support. World Wars I and II were popular because people believed that the survival of America's democratic institutions was at stake. In both wars, the American people rallied with an enthusiasm and spirit of self-sacrifice that was remarkable for a country with such a diverse population. Support for food and fuel rationing, the purchase of war bonds, a high rate of voluntary enlistments, and countless other forms of voluntarism, were characteristic of the people's response to those wars. Most recently, the Persian Gulf War prompted an unprecedented show of support even though the United States was not directly threatened by the conflict. Rallies in support of U.S. troops were widespread. Tens of thousands of individuals, including families, friends, and well-wishers of the troops sent packages of food, cosmetics, clothes, cassettes, and suntan oil. And even more supporters wrote letters to unknown soldiers that were forwarded to the military front. In fact, most public opinion polls revealed that up to 90 percent of all Americans approved of their nation's involvement.

The complex interplay of events and purposes that leads to military conflict should be included in a history of any war. A simple chronicling of battles and casualty lists at best offers only a partial history of war. Wars do not spontaneously erupt; nor does their memory perish. They are driven by underlying causes, fueled by policy-makers, fought and supported by citizens, and remembered by those plotting a nation's future. For these reasons wars, or the fear of wars, will always leave an indelible stamp on any nation's history and influence its future.

The purpose of this series is to provide a full understanding of America's Wars by presenting each war in a historical context. Each of the twelve volumes focuses on the events that led up to the war, the war itself, its impact on the home front, and its aftermath and influence upon future conflicts. The unique personalities, the dramatic acts of courage and compassion, as well as the despair and horror of war are all presented in this series. Together, they show why America's wars have dominated American consciousness in the past as well as how they guide many political decisions of today. In these vivid and objective accounts, students will gain an understanding of why America became involved in these conflicts, and how historians, military and government officials, and others have come to understand and interpret that involvement.

Chronology of Events

1860

November Abraham Lincoln is elected the sixteenth president.

December South Carolina convention votes to secede.

1861

January Mississippi, Florida, Alabama, Georgia, and Louisiana secede.

February Texas secedes. Jefferson Davis is inaugurated as president of the Confederate States of America.

March Lincoln is inaugurated.

April 12 Confederates fire on Fort Sumter, off the coast of South Carolina. Civil War begins.

May Arkansas, Tennessee, North Carolina, and Virginia secede.

July 21 First Battle of Bull Run in Virginia.

November George McClellan is named general in chief of Union armies.

Black slaves return home from the cotton fields. The Civil War brought an end to slavery.

Abraham Lincoln is inaugurated in 1861. During the Civil War, Lincoln was an unpopular leader.

1862

March 9 Battle between the *Monitor* and the *Merrimac*.

April 6–7 Battle of Shiloh in Tennessee.

June 31 Robert E. Lee is appointed to command the Army of Northern Virginia.

June 25–July 1 Battles of the Seven Days in Virginia.

August 29–30 Second Battle of Bull Run.

September 17 Battle of Antietam in Maryland.

November 7 Ambrose Burnside replaces McClellan as commander of the Army of the Potomac.

December 13 Battle of Fredericksburg in Virginia.

1863

January 1 Lincoln signs Emancipation Proclamation.

January 26 Joseph Hooker replaces Burnside as commander of the Army of the Potomac.

May 1–4   Battle of Chancellorsville in Virginia.

May 10   Stonewall Jackson dies.

June 28   George Meade replaces Hooker as commander of the Army of the Potomac.

July 1–3   Battle of Gettysburg in Pennsylvania.

July 4   Confederate fort at Vicksburg, Mississippi, surrenders to Ulysses S. Grant.

November 19   Lincoln delivers the Gettysburg Address.

1864

March 12   Grant is named general in chief of Union armies.

June 1–3   Battle of Cold Harbor in Virginia.

July 22   Battle of Atlanta in Georgia.

September   Union troops occupy Atlanta.

November 8   Lincoln is reelected president.

November 15   William Tecumseh Sherman begins march to the sea from Atlanta to Savannah, Georgia.

Union and Confederate soldiers fight during the siege of Vicksburg. Civil War soldiers' sophisticated weapons resulted in a high number of casualties.

1865

January 31   Congress submits Thirteenth Amendment, abolishing slavery.

April 2   Petersburg, Virginia, falls to Union troops.

April 3   Union troops occupy Richmond, Virginia.

April 9   Lee surrenders to Grant at Appomattox Court House, Virginia.

April 14   Lincoln is assassinated.

The Battle of Shiloh was one of the bloodiest of the war. Here, corpses fill Bloody Lane, the site of some of the fiercest fighting.

The Bloodiest War

No war has had a more profound effect on the United States of America than the Civil War. Its outcome not only determined the political future of the country but also how American society would develop. The outcome of the Civil War has affected almost every American living today.

Between April 1861 and April 1865, the Civil War claimed 620,000 American lives, more than the combined deaths from all the other wars the United States has fought. At a time when the nation's population was only 30 million, that meant 1 out of every 50 Americans was killed in this war, or about 1 out of every 12 men and boys between the ages of fifteen and fifty.

More than half of the soldiers who were not killed were either wounded or taken prisoner. In small Northern and Southern towns after the war, crippled men were seen on every street and sidewalk. Some had lost an arm; others were missing a leg or both legs. Some towns had only a few young or middle-aged men after the war. Army regiments in those days were made up of men from the same geographic region, and in a single bloody battle, such as those at Shiloh, Antietam, or Gettysburg, all the soldiers from one town might be wiped out.

The names of these and other battles are etched deeply into the American memory. Few events have touched Americans as deeply—or have roused such mixed emotions—as the Civil War. While half of the country rejoiced at General Grant's victories in Virginia, the other half felt the sadness of General Lee's surrender. The celebration of the restoration of the Union was cut short by the assassination of President Abraham Lincoln. Every casualty was an American casualty. Every farm, village, town, and city damaged by this war was an American one, and every family torn apart by the war was an American family.

In a war filled with ironies, the greatest irony may have been the role played by four million black slaves. It was their differences over slavery that drove the two halves of the United States to war. Yet the Civil War did not start as a war to end slavery. At first, Lincoln did not even intend to end slavery if the North won the war. Rather, he wanted to force the Confederate states—Virginia, North Carolina, South Carolina, Georgia, Florida, Tennessee, Alabama, Mississippi, Arkansas, Louisiana, and Texas—to rejoin the Union. That was all. He even gave the slave owners in these states repeated assurances that he would not abolish slavery there.

It was not until New Year's Day, 1863, that Lincoln issued the Emancipation Proclamation and the war became a war to abolish slavery. Shortly after the Civil War came to a close in April 1865, the Thirteenth Amendment to the Constitution abolished slavery everywhere in the country. Although this officially ended the fight over slavery, North and South remained as emotionally divided as ever.

The first sign of this division was the assassination of Abraham Lincoln by a Southern secessionist just five days after the war ended. Following the assassination, the mood among most Northerners turned from triumph to vengeance. They wanted to punish the South and strip its leaders of any present or future

A young soldier stares out at the camera. Many of the soldiers that fought in the Civil War were little more than boys. (Below) The original caption for this engraving read: The peculiar "Domestic Institutions of our Southern brethren."

Years after the Civil War, Southerners could not forget the terrible destruction Union troops wreaked upon their cities. Here a depot in Charleston, South Carolina, lies in ruins.

political power. The result was Reconstruction, the period from 1865 to 1875, when Northern administrators supervised the rebuilding of state governments in the South.

Southerners were powerless to resist this method of reconstruction. Their state governments were dissolved, their economy was in shambles, and their land was devastated by the war. Farms and plantations had no one to work them, and almost every Southern family grieved for the loss of at least one loved one. To Southerners, the North was unduly harsh, vindictive, and insensitive. These feelings remained in the hearts and minds of Southerners for generations to come. In addition, the end of slavery did not mean the end of racism and poor treatment of blacks. It would take more than the Civil War to bring about true freedom for blacks.

Today, memorials of the Civil War and of the soldiers who fought in it mark the American landscape from Maine to Texas. The gravestones of 620,000 Yankee and Rebel soldiers fill our cemeteries. The modern United States—its government, its laws, and its people—is a product of that conflict. More than 100 million black and white Americans living in every part of the country have ancestors who fought in the Civil War, who were emancipated from slavery through the Civil War, or who were forced to free their slaves as a result of that war. The Civil War shaped their lives, their society, their nation, and through them, it has shaped us.

CHAPTER ONE

The Roots of War

From the earliest days of nationhood, rivalries between the northern and the southern parts of the United States helped shape the U.S. government and fashion its laws. With different geographies and climates, the North and the South developed very different economies and life-styles. Following the American Revolution, the North was almost immediately immersed in another revolution—an industrial revolution. With excellent harbors and waterways, Northern cities like New York, Philadelphia, Pittsburgh, Boston, Providence, Portland, Detroit, and Chicago became centers of the industrial and commercial revolution. New factories were built to make clothing, tools, guns, bricks, concrete, glass, and steel to build bridges, railroad tracks, and train cars. Virtually every other manufactured item was also produced in these factories.

The Northern cities became the world's "melting pot" as immigrants streamed to the United States from Ireland, Italy, Germany, and other European nations to work in the new factories, shipyards, mills, and mines. Between 1850 and 1860, five million Europeans immigrated to the United States, raising the nation's population to thirty million. The vast majority of immigrants found work in the increasingly crowded, noisy, bustling Northern cities.

In the industrialized North, the expansion of businesses presented white people with great opportunities for success. Most Northerners believed that with intelligence and hard work, any white male had a chance to make a fortune. Many successful business owners, lawyers, doctors, and politicians were products

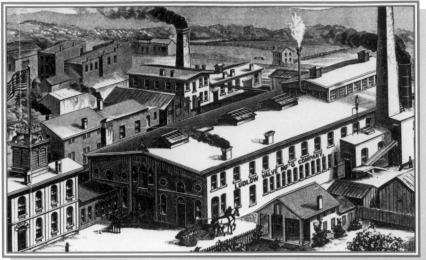

Northern cities became increasingly industrialized during the 1850s and 1860s. Immigrants quickly filled the many jobs offered by the new factories in the North.

of this free labor system. Abraham Lincoln, who was born in a log cabin and worked as a rail-splitter in his youth, eventually became a national symbol of this "American dream." And there were thousands of other examples of people who had made their fortune by inventing something or investing their earnings in their own business ventures.

The Life-style of the Southern Plantation Owner

The South, on the other hand, was not affected by the industrial revolution. It proudly retained its rural character as a realm of small towns and picturesque villages nestled among ample forests, rivers, and streams. The South developed an economy that relied not on factory production but on the production of cash crops grown on huge farms called plantations.

Fields of cotton, rice, tobacco, and sugar were grown on plantations. Among the fields stood the plantation owner's stately mansion with its elegant pillars and wide verandas. A plantation was usually owned by a single, powerful family who enjoyed an elegant life-style in the tradition of European nobility.

The work on these huge farms—planting, harvesting, looking after the plantation house, and attending to the needs of the owner and his family—required a tremendous amount of labor. To supply that labor, plantation owners depended almost entirely on black slaves. The slaves, who worked from sunrise to sunset and lived in run-down huts called shanties, were not allowed to leave the plantation. They were bought, sold, and traded like livestock, and many were treated more like animals than human beings.

Genes, Not Hard Work, the Key to Success

In the South, achieving wealth and success depended more than anything else on one's family. A small minority of wealthy landowners governed the land and the laws in the South. Most members of this wealthy ruling class were convinced that they were genetically and morally superior not only to blacks but to other whites.

Wealthy landowners believed they were descendants of the noble counts and barons of Europe. A true Southern gentleman was supposed to act like a dashing and gallant soldier. He should be an excellent horseman, swordsman, and lady's man. The aristocratic Southern lady was taught to be charming, elegant, and extremely delicate.

In contrast to the industrialized North, the American South was rural and depended on manual labor to harvest and plant crops. Almost all of this labor was performed by black slaves (below).

Life on a Plantation

A large Southern plantation was self-sufficient. Practically all the food needed by the owner's family and their slaves was grown and prepared on the plantation, which usually had its own stockyards, butcher shops, smokehouses, gardens, grain mills, blacksmith shops, seamstress quarters, and storehouses. These buildings flanked the "big house," where the owner's family lived.

Serving the plantation owner's family in the big house were house slaves. These servants, maids, and butlers were usually treated better than the field slaves. They were often taught to read and write so that they could understand written instructions. They were slaves nevertheless, with no more rights than their brothers and sisters who worked the fields.

With house slaves to wait on them, the owner's family often enjoyed a luxurious lifestyle. The plantation house usually featured the finest in contemporary comfort and elegance. Furniture was often imported from France, crystal and silver from England or Germany.

Forty or fifty slaves lived on a typical plantation. Besides house slaves and field slaves, some slaves were trained to be blacksmiths, carpenters, seamstresses, or butchers. Nothing could have been in greater contrast to the slave owner's lifestyle than the living conditions of his slaves. Between six and twelve slaves lived together in a leaky, drafty, dirt-floored, one-room shack. These slave cabins bred malaria and other diseases that claimed thousands of lives each year. Most slaves suffered from worms, dysentery, and rotten teeth. They were poorly fed, usually existing on a "hog and hominy" diet that consisted of a little corn and about three pounds of fatty pork a week. They wore shabby clothes made of homespun cotton known as "Negro cloth." Slave children often went barefoot year-round until they were old enough to work in the fields.

By 1850, there were four million black slaves in the South. Approximately one out of every three people living in the South was a slave. Most of them lived in a state of constant squalor and terror. The threat of the rawhide whip kept most slaves in line. Slaves who refused to work or attempted to escape were whipped until the skin was ripped off their backs. Repeat offenders received more severe punishment. Some were forced to wear a leg iron permanently attached to one ankle. Sometimes, the leg was rubbed so raw that it became infected and had to be amputated. Such surgery was usually performed on slaves without an anesthetic to block the pain. Punishments varied from owner to owner.

Despite the awful dangers of getting caught and being punished, some slaves tried to escape to the North. To track down runaway slaves, plantation owners often hired professional slave hunters armed with teams of bloodhounds. Sympathetic whites living on both sides of the Mason-Dixon line helped fugitive slaves hide and eventually escape into the North. This route to freedom was known as the underground railroad. One underground railroad worker was Harriet Tubman, an escaped slave who dedicated her life to helping other slaves get out of the South.

"I'd rather be dead than be a nigger on one of these big plantations," a white Mississippi farmer told a Northern visitor. Perhaps this farmer would have considered it a blessing that most slaves died young. Fewer than four out of one hundred lived to be sixty years old.

From the age of twelve, slaves were expected to get up at sunrise and work until it was too dark to see. They were watched by an overseer, whose cracking whip reminded them not to stop working until he told them to. One unknown slave's words sum up the plight of all slaves: "No day ever dawns for the slave. Nor is it looked for. For the slave it is all night—all night forever."

In contrast, many working-class and poor whites in the South were uneducated. Many of them could not even pass the literacy tests that were required before they could vote. So democracy in the South was restricted to the wealthy minority. Only white males who could read and write were allowed to vote.

As a result, almost all Southern political leaders were slaveholders. They not only controlled political issues in the South but they had an unusual amount of power in Washington. Although the slave states were less populous than the Northern states, each slave state had two senators in Congress, just like every other state. The Southern senators were a formidable group that could stop just about any legislative action that it did not like.

The Slave Power

The Southern slaveholders, therefore, gave the South enormous political clout. In fact, before the election of Abraham Lincoln in 1860, no president had ever been elected without the support of this group. Northerners resented this power. They referred to the slave owners, who made up an extremely small minority of the national population, as the "slave power."

The interests of the slave power were often opposed to those of the Northern industrialists—workers and owners alike. Northern workers considered themselves free to sell their labor or to withhold it as they saw fit. They were free to accept, decline, or quit any job. As they worked to establish their rights to fair wages and decent working conditions, Northerners viewed slavery and the Southern plantation system as symbols of economic tyranny.

Another way the North and South differed politically was in their attitudes toward the role of the federal government. The South opposed most government-sponsored community improvements. While a majority of Northerners supported the investment of government money in public schools, banks, railroads, and canals, most Southerners did not. The Northerners supported the Whig party, which was in favor of these public projects, and the Southerners supported the conservative Democratic party. This was the party that supported states' rights and strict limits on the powers of the federal government.

Public Education

A major split between North and South was over public education. The North supported free public schools. Horace Mann, a founder of the public school system in Massachusetts, claimed that schools were "more powerful in the production and gainful employment of the total wealth of a country than all the other things mentioned in the books of the political economists." A wealthy

A typical Southern plantation. Plantation owners owed their wealth to the cheap labor provided by their slaves.

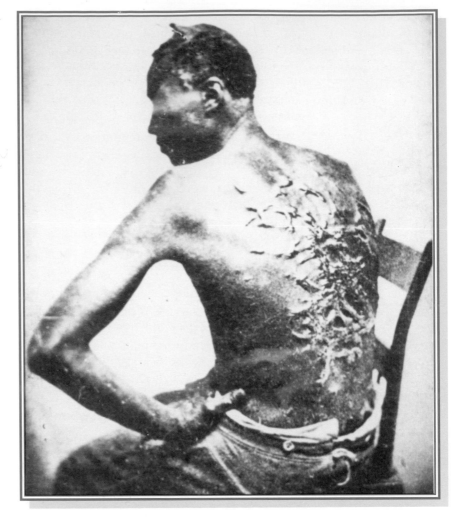

A hideous web of scars is testimony to the severe beatings this black slave endured. During the war, this man escaped and fought as a soldier in the Union army.

manufacturer in Virginia who wanted his state to imitate the North's school system said, "You cannot expect to develop your resources without a general system of popular education. It is the lever to all permanent improvement." Most Yankee businesspeople echoed this view. "Intelligent laborers can add much more to the capital employed in a business than those who are ignorant," said one.

But Southern politicians and plantation owners disagreed. They wanted to maintain the differences between the rich and the poor. Plantation owners had no desire to see the working classes educated. One of them asked, "Is this the way to produce producers? To make every child in the state a literary character would not be a good qualification for those who must live by manual labor." If the working classes were educated, they would want to improve their standard of living, perhaps even challenge the slaveholders' power. Southern plantation owners thought that by keeping the working classes ignorant, they could control them.

Westward Expansion

Because of these differences, distrust and disagreement grew between the North and the South. Yet the two regions would probably have continued to tolerate one another if it had not been for westward expansion. The new territories acquired through the Louisiana Purchase and later through the conquest of former Mexican territory in Texas, New Mexico, and California meant that more states would surely join the nation. As each new state was formed, it would enter the Union either as a free state or a slave state.

New States and Slavery

Whether new territories applying for statehood would develop the free labor system of the North or follow the traditional slave economy of the South was the issue that really divided the nation.

The struggle began in 1819, when the Missouri Territory sought statehood. At that time, slavery was illegal in exactly half of the nation's twenty-two states and legal in the other half. When the people of Missouri voted by a narrow margin to permit slavery, it fueled a controversy. Northern congressmen did not want to upset the balance of power between free and slave states. So the House of Representatives passed a bill declaring that Missouri could enter the Union only if it banned slavery.

Southerners in the Senate, led by the fiery South Carolinian John C. Calhoun, claimed that this was a violation of states' rights. They believed that each state had the right to determine whether or not to allow slavery. Southern senators also feared that if Missouri entered the Union as a free state, the free states would have a majority in both houses of Congress. That could give opponents of slavery an opportunity to abolish the practice in the South.

Henry Clay's Compromise of 1850 postponed a war between the North and South for nearly a decade. Clay also ran as a presidential candidate five times and lost each time. This lack of success once caused him to declare that he "would rather be right than be President."

The Missouri Compromise

In 1820, Congressman Henry Clay of Kentucky hammered out a compromise that was accepted by both the Senate and the House of Representatives. Missouri would be admitted as a slave state, but Maine would join as a free state at the same time. This would retain the balance of free states and slave states in the Senate. In addition, however, the South won a major concession. Congress agreed that the southern border of Missouri would become a dividing line and Slavery would be permitted anywhere south of this line. The compromise became known as the Missouri Compromise. For nearly thirty years, it helped keep peace between the North and the South.

The Abolitionists

Organized opposition to slavery began in 1831 when William Lloyd Garrison of Boston founded the abolitionist newspaper *The Liberator.* Garrison called on opponents of slavery to take steps to end this great social evil. Many of the early abolitionists were New England clergymen, and Boston became the unofficial headquarters of the abolition movement. In addition to Garrison, Rev. Thomas Parker, Wendell Phillips, Salmon P. Chase, Frederick Douglass, Harriet Beecher Stowe, and many other leaders of the movement were from Boston.

The abolitionists organized antislavery parades, parlor meetings, and church committees to spread their message. They formed groups to help slaves escape to Northern cities and to protect runaway slaves from slave hunters. The abolitionists never represented the view of the majority of Americans, but in the years just before and during the Civil War, they had an enormous influence on the Republican party, which gained control of Congress in 1860.

Frederick Douglass (right), William Lloyd Garrison (center), and Salmon P. Chase (left) were in favor of abolishing slavery. At first, abolitionist views were considered too radical to the average American. But slowly, Northerners began to question slavery's morality and purpose.

But the peace wrought by the Missouri Compromise was an uneasy peace. When Southern slave hunters came into Northern cities to track down runaway slaves, Northern resentment and opposition to slavery increased. The membership of the antislavery, or abolitionist, groups swelled, and the cry to abolish slavery was heard throughout the North. The writings of William Lloyd Garrison, founder of the abolitionist newspaper *The Liberator,* described the horrors of slavery. He called on other abolitionists to form committees to help hide and protect runaway, or fugitive, slaves.

The Greatest Evil

To many Northern educators, religious leaders, and political leaders, the greatest social sin was slavery. These leaders viewed the South as a backward society dependent on the evil, archaic institution of slavery. According to them, slavery was undermining Southern society and leading it to ruin. William Henry Seward, a leader of the predominantly Northern Whig party, claimed that the institution of slavery had made Southerners lazy. It had led, he said, to "an exhausted soil, old and decaying towns, wretchedly-neglected roads, an absence of enterprise and improvement."

In his most famous antislavery speech, Seward deplored slavery as "incompatible with all the elements of the security, welfare, and greatness of nations." He continued, "Slavery and free labor are antagonistic systems between which rages an irrepressible conflict" that must lead to the destruction of slavery.

The Southern View of Slavery

In the South, slaveholders were angered by the North's depiction of them as masters of an immoral society. Many slaveholders agreed with Sen. Albert Brown of Mississippi that slavery was "a great moral, social, and political blessing—a blessing to the slave, and a blessing to the master." They claimed that it had civilized the African savages and provided them with security "from the cradle to the grave."

In addition, slaveholders believed that slavery elevated the status of all white people by releasing them from menial labor and protecting them from degrading competition for jobs with freed blacks. Finally, slavery was the foundation on which the upper class of gentlemen and ladies was built. Because slaves did most of the physical labor on the plantations, the owners had time to cultivate the arts, literature, and hospitality. Sen. Robert Hunter of Virginia even made the bold claim that "there

The Slave Trade

Every slave could expect to be sold at least once in his or her lifetime, and slave owners did not care about keeping husbands and wives—or even parents and children—together. The traditional wedding vow "Till death do us part" was modified for slaves to "Till death or distance do us part." Slaves were usually sold at auctions, like livestock. On the auction block, they were poked and prodded, made to jump or dance, and stripped to reveal how often they had been whipped. Numerous whippings were a sign of disobedience, which drastically lowered a slave's value.

A Southern leaflet announces the auction of slaves and other items.

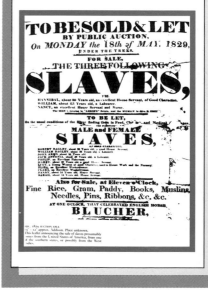

Uncle Tom's Cabin

Anger over the Fugitive Slave Law of 1850 led to rapid growth of the abolitionist movement, but nothing caused its ranks to swell as much as *Uncle Tom's Cabin,* a novel written in 1852 by Harriet Beecher Stowe.

First published serially in an abolitionist newspaper, the *National Era, Uncle Tom's Cabin* was not anti-South and, in fact, presented some favorable aspects of slavery. Nevertheless, scenes that depicted slaves running for their freedom or enduring beatings made slavery an emotional issue for hundreds of thousands of Americans. It influenced teachers, writers, and politicians both here and abroad. It is difficult to measure the political influence of a piece of fiction, but Lord Palmerston, who became prime minister of England a decade later, credited Stowe's novel for helping him decide against recognizing the Confederacy as an independent nation. When Abraham Lincoln was grappling with the issue of emancipation a decade later, he reread *Uncle Tom's Cabin* and borrowed from the Library of Congress Stowe's *A Key to "Uncle Tom's Cabin,"* which documented her research on slavery. When Lincoln met Stowe later that same year, he commented, "So you're the little woman who wrote the book that made this great war."

is not a respectable system of civilization known to history whose foundations were not laid in the institution of domestic slavery."

Most Northerners had little hope of abolishing slavery in the South. But they did not want slavery to spread into western territories. If slavery gained a foothold in the West, it would not only obstruct free labor there but it would give the slave power a chance to control the Senate. If that happened, many Northerners even feared that slavery might once again become legal in the North.

Two Separate Nations?

Southerners, for their part, felt equally threatened. With California and parts of the New Mexico Territory ready to join the Union as free states in 1850, the slave power feared losing its grip on the federal government. If that happened, Southerners would be at the mercy of the North. Proud Southern gentlemen could not envision living in a country ruled by Northern peasants. John C. Calhoun, now old and frail and suffering so badly from tuberculosis that a colleague had to read his speeches for him, called for Congress to adopt a slave charter, granting slaveholders equal rights in all new territories. He also demanded that Northern states guarantee the return of runaway slaves to their owners. If these things could not be guaranteed, then the South and North should separate into two countries and govern themselves in peace, Calhoun proposed.

Northerners were shocked by Calhoun's message, but in the South many landowners greeted it with wild enthusiasm. They believed that seceding from the Union might be the only way to preserve their way of life. Henry Clay, the Kentucky senator who had forged the Missouri Compromise thirty years earlier, once again became the voice of moderation. Like Calhoun, Clay was an ailing statesman in his last years of service. In January 1850, he proposed that California be admitted as a free state but, at the same time, laws be passed to protect the rights of slave states.

Clay's proposal was victorious. The Compromise of 1850 was enacted in September of that year. California became the nation's thirty-first state, and it prohibited slavery. But at the same time, the Fugitive Slave Law was passed, which gave Southern slaveholders the right to cross state borders to hunt and capture runaway slaves in the North.

Many Southerners were appeased. Even the *Charleston* (SC) *Mercury* newspaper, a strong voice in favor of slavery and states' rights, praised Clay's efforts: "With such a spirit of compromise, it no longer seems impossible to bring this sectional contest to a close."

Abraham Lincoln called Harriet Beecher Stowe "the little woman that made this great war." In Uncle Tom's Cabin, *she voiced the feelings many Northerners had about slavery.*

Uncle Tom's Cabin

Antislavery groups in the North were outraged by the Compromise of 1850, and especially by the Fugitive Slave Law. In 1852, Harriet Beecher Stowe published *Uncle Tom's Cabin,* a novel about the oppression and mistreatment of slaves. Within four years, the novel had sold more copies than any other book in the United States except the Bible. One person moved by this novel and other antislavery literature was Abraham Lincoln, a congressman from Illinois who spoke out passionately against slavery: "On this point hold firm, as with a chain of steel. Those who deny freedom to others deserve it not for themselves. And under a just God, cannot long retain it."

In the meantime, more western territories were preparing for statehood. One of these was Kansas, which lay north of the Mason-Dixon line. Many slave owners from the South had moved into Kansas and brought their slaves with them.

Technically, the Missouri Compromise of 1820 prohibited slavery in this area, but a group of congressmen led by Democratic senator Stephen Douglas of Illinois made the issue of slavery in Kansas a test of states' rights. They declared that states should be able to decide for themselves whether to allow slavery. After fierce debate, Congress went along with Douglas and enacted the Kansas-Nebraska Act of 1854. This act repealed the Missouri Compromise and allowed slavery to exist in any territory where it had not been abolished by a direct vote of the people living there.

Bloody Kansas

As people moved into Kansas to settle that territory, confrontations erupted between slave owners and their opponents. The Kansas-Nebraska Act of 1854 allowed the settlers in these two territories to decide for themselves whether they would allow slavery to exist. The majority would rule. Slave owners therefore convinced proslavery settlers from the neighboring state of Missouri, a slave state, to settle in Kansas. Some of them were genuine settlers, but others were simply hired to raise the number of voters in favor of slavery. Many of these hired men, known as border ruffians, used or threatened to use violence to persuade other settlers to vote for slavery. Groups of border ruffians rode through the state, raiding the homes and burning the fields of "free staters," those who opposed slavery.

Many free staters armed themselves with rifles and outdated artillery from the Mexican War to fight the border ruffians. New Englanders who opposed slavery went to Kansas to help the free staters. As a result of these confrontations, Kansas in the 1850s became known as "bloody Kansas," where more than two hundred men died fighting over slavery. The willingness to fight over slavery would not end in Kansas. Soon these differences would lead the North and the South closer to an unavoidable collision. A strong political movement to stop the spread of slavery was emerging in the North. As it gained strength, it drove the North closer to war with the South.

CHAPTER TWO

An Unavoidable Conflict

The antislavery groups that broke away from the Whig party in the 1850s formed several splinter groups. The largest of these was called the Free Soil Party. In 1856, the Free Soilers called a convention in Philadelphia "for all who are opposed to the repeal of the Missouri Compromise and to the policy of the present administration." By the time the gathering convened in June, all the parties sending delegates were referring to the convention as a gathering of "republicans."

This was the birth of the Republican party. Its first candidate for president was John Charles Fremont, a California explorer. The Republicans attracted the nation's best-known opponents of slavery, including Sen. William Henry Seward and Congressman Abraham Lincoln. Leaders of the new party appealed to moderate Northerners. They were careful not to align themselves too closely with the abolitionists. They did not call for the abolition of slavery in states where it already existed. Instead, their platform in the 1856 presidential election called for the prohibition of slavery in all U.S. territories and new states.

Although Fremont was soundly defeated by Democrat James Buchanan, the Republicans replaced the Whigs as the majority party in the North, and they showed that an antislavery platform could win in the North. But in the South, hatred for the Republicans was almost universal.

The Democratic party took advantage of this strong anti-Republican sentiment and built a coalition of Northern and Southern Democrats. One of their most effective positions, in both the North and the South, was the Democratic stand on race.

If the Republicans gained power, warned the Democrats, they would emancipate blacks throughout the country, and the North would soon be overrun by four million uneducated former slaves.

An Atmosphere of Fear

The Democrats exploited every possible fear of a free black population. They warned that blacks would be willing to work for extremely low wages and would steal jobs from working-class whites. If blacks were given citizenship and equal rights, they would elect black mayors and legislators, who would then run the government. If being governed by blacks were not enough to frighten voters, the Democrats told mothers and fathers that their daughters would be forced to marry black men.

Many Americans believed these threats. Even among people who opposed slavery, racial prejudice was strong. Only a minority of Americans believed that freed blacks should be able to vote and enjoy all the rights of citizenship. Just a handful of New England states had given blacks these rights.

Dred Scott

Fear of and discrimination against blacks was so strong that many abolitionists believed it would take more than Republicans in Congress to free slaves and grant them equality. An event that occurred in 1857 convinced them that they were right. That event was a Supreme Court decision involving a slave named Dred Scott.

Dred Scott was a Missouri slave who sued his new owners for freedom after his master died in 1843. Scott claimed that he should be set free because he had lived with his former master for many years on free soil in Illinois and Wisconsin. The court, dominated by Southern justices, decided that Scott was not protected by the Constitution because he was black.

Chief Justice Roger Taney, a Southerner, wrote that "at the time the Constitution was written, Negroes were regarded as so far inferior that they had no rights which the white man was bound to respect." The Supreme Court sided with the slave owners. A slave was property, and the Fifth Amendment guaranteed that no American citizen should "be deprived of life, liberty or property." The court decided that blacks were not citizens.

Although this Supreme Court decision upheld the rights of slaveholders, it created such a reaction throughout the North and South that in the end, it may have hurt Southerners more than it helped them. Many Southern leaders overreacted to the Supreme Court decision. They interpreted it to mean that all prohibitions against slavery were unconstitutional. They now sought to pass a bill in Congress that would establish a national slave code, legalizing slavery in all existing and future U.S. territories.

Free and Slave States and Territories (1861)

WASHINGTON TERRITORY

OREGON 1859

MINNESOTA 1858

DAKOTA TERRITORY

WISCONSIN

MICHIGAN

MAINE

VT.

NEW YORK

N.H.
MASS.
R.I.
CONN.

NEVADA TERRITORY

UTAH TERRITORY

NEBRASKA TERRITORY

IOWA

PENN.

N.J.
MASON-DIXON LINE
DEL.
MD.

CALIFORNIA

COLORADO TERRITORY

KANSAS 1861

ILLINOIS

INDIANA

OHIO

MISSOURI

VIRGINIA

PUBLIC LAND

KENTUCKY

NEW MEXICO TERRITORY

INDIAN TERRITORY

ARKANSAS

TENNESSEE

NORTH CAROLINA

SOUTH CAROLINA

TEXAS

MISSISSIPPI

ALABAMA

GEORGIA

LOUISIANA

FLORIDA

FREE STATES

SLAVE STATES

OPEN TO SLAVERY BY DRED SCOTT DECISION (1857)

President James Buchanan disapproved of slavery, but felt that under the Constitution states and new territories had the right to decide whether to enter the Union as slave states.

As with so many slavery issues, this one reached its boiling point in Kansas. In 1858, a corrupt, proslavery territorial government convened a special statehood convention in Lecompton, Kansas, to draft a state constitution. The convention was organized by proslavery leaders, and it was boycotted by the antislavery forces. Not surprisingly, the delegates drafted a constitution that permitted slavery. The next step was to hold a voter referendum to approve the constitution.

When the Lecompton constitution was submitted to Kansas voters for approval, most Republicans and "free soilers" called the referendum a farce because the coalition that had drafted it represented a small, corrupt minority. The Republicans refused to participate in the statewide referendum. This allowed the constitution to pass by a vote of 6,226 to 569, and Kansas submitted its constitution to Congress. Although its bid to enter the Union as a slave state was clearly an undemocratic maneuver supported by a pro-Southern minority, it received the support of President James Buchanan, a pro-Southern Democrat. The Senate, with its strong Southern power bloc, voted to grant Kansas statehood.

John Brown: Martyr of the Abolition Movement

One of the most radical abolitionists was John Brown. Brown preached that the sin of slavery could be purged only with bloodshed. When it became clear to Brown that slavery would not be abolished in his home state of Kansas, he made plans to bring the slaves together in a general uprising against their owners. In 1859, he appealed to William Lloyd Garrison, to black leader Frederick Douglass, and to other leaders of the struggle against slavery to help him raise an army of abolitionists. With this army, he planned to raid the U.S. Army arsenal at Harpers Ferry, Virginia, then use the weapons from the arsenal to liberate the slaves from Virginia plantations. He expected the freed slaves to lead the slave rebellion. Following their victory, he intended to establish a black state with its own government somewhere in the South. Douglass, who had escaped from slavery himself as a teenager and had become

John Brown as a young man. A self-styled angel of the Lord, Brown believed that slavery was an intolerable injustice.

one of the most eloquent and convincing black spokesmen for equal rights, tried to persuade Brown that attacking a U.S. Army installation was insane. He refused to join Brown's army, as did Garrison and other abolitionist leaders. While they admired his conviction, they believed it was a suicidal mission.

So on the rainy, cold Sunday night of October 16, 1859, Brown led a small band—including his four sons, four free blacks, one escaped slave, and about a dozen abolitionists—across the Potomac River into Harpers Ferry. There, they captured the arsenal and took several hostages. Brown expected news of this bold maneuver to incite thousands of slaves to escape and rally to his side at the arsenal, but that did not happen.

Within hours, the townspeople of Harpers Ferry surrounded the raiders. The next morning, they were joined by several companies of Virginia's volunteer militia. Outnumbered by more than twenty to one, Brown's ragtag army fought on all day. Three of Brown's black followers were shot down while trying to flee from the arsenal. The townspeople hung two of the bodies up for target practice, cutting off the ears and other extremities for souvenirs. The third body was thrown to the hogs. By nightfall, six more of Brown's raiders were dead, and two of his sons lay wounded. His son Oliver begged him either to surrender or to kill him and end his misery. "If you must die, die like a man," his father replied coldly.

When old John Brown looked out from the arsenal the following morning, October 18, two thousand soldiers of the U.S. Army had joined the fight against him. They were led by Lt. Comdr. Robert E. Lee, who sent his aide, Lt. Jeb Stuart, to demand Brown's surrender. Brown refused to surrender, and Lieutenant Stuart signaled his troops to storm the arsenal. Within minutes, only Brown and six of his men were still alive. Severely wounded, Brown finally surrendered.

Six days later, he was sentenced to hang. On December 2, 1859, old John Brown was led to the hanging scaffold at Charles Town, Virginia. In attendance at the hanging was a professor from the Virginia Military Institute named Thomas J. Jackson, who two years later would earn the nickname "Stonewall." Also in the crowd that day was a handsome young cadet from Richmond, Virginia, by the name of John Wilkes Booth.

On the scaffold, Brown did not ask forgiveness or utter a sound. Instead, he handed a note to a guard, on which he had written this somber warning: "I, John Brown, am now quite certain that the crimes of this guilty land will never be purged away but with blood."

Overnight, John Brown became a martyr of the abolition movement. His name became synonymous with the slaves' struggle for freedom, and an anonymously written song named "John Brown's Body" became virtually an anthem of the movement, sung at meetings and rallies across the North. A few years later, Julia Ward Howe used the tune from this song to accompany the words to her "Battle Hymn of the Republic."

Frederick Douglass praised Brown as a hero who died trying to make slaves free: "His zeal in the cause of freedom was infinitely superior to mine. Mine was like the taper light; his was as the burning sun. I could live for the slaves; John Brown could die for them."

Not all opponents of slavery considered Brown a hero. Abraham Lincoln, who was frequently being mentioned as the next Republican candidate for president, condemned Brown's criminal actions and supported his execution: "Old John Brown has been executed for treason against a state. We cannot object, even though he agreed with us in thinking slavery wrong. That cannot excuse violence, bloodshed, and treason. It could avail him nothing that he might think himself right."

Whether regarded as a martyr, a madman, or a criminal, John Brown could not be ignored. Author Herman Melville called Brown "the meteor of the war." Melville may have been right, but if Brown's actions did bring on the war, it was not in the way Brown had envisioned. Rather than inspiring slaves and abolitionists to take up arms, his raid on Harpers Ferry forced the Virginia militia into duty for the first time since the Revolution. Now, other state governments in the South took steps to arm and train their militia and put them on alert in case of future slave uprisings. These units were to become the initial corps of the Confederate army.

In this dramatic mural, John Brown is depicted as a holy warrior with a holy book in one hand and a gun in the other.

Stephen Douglas (above) was a masterful orator who defended the principle of states' rights. (Below) Stephen Douglas and Abraham Lincoln debate the merits of slavery versus states' rights in this artist's representation of their famous discussions.

One senator who did not vote in its favor was Stephen Douglas. If he had supported bringing Kansas into the Union as a slave state, the South would have embraced him as a hero and he would have almost certainly been the Democratic presidential nominee in 1860. Douglas, however, did not hesitate to vote his conviction. "I could never vote," he told his fellow lawmakers, "to force this constitution down the throats of the people of Kansas, in opposition to their wishes and in violation of our pledges." As a party leader, Douglas influenced many Northern Democrats in the House of Representatives. When the petition for statehood was rejected by the House, Douglas became a hero overnight among Northerners and was considered a traitor by Southerners.

The inability to get Kansas into the Union as a slave state was a devastating loss for the South, but perhaps not as devastating as the division it caused within the Democratic party. On one side were the Southern Democrats, who insisted that any individual had the right to own slaves. On the other side, Douglas and most Northern Democrats believed that a state had as much right to prohibit slavery as to permit it. This division in the Democratic party seriously weakened Douglas's chances of becoming the next president. In fact, it weakened the chance that any Democrat could gather enough support to become president.

For Douglas, there was another, more immediate hurdle to overcome in his political career. He faced reelection to the Senate from

The Lincoln-Douglas Debates

Although millions of Northerners carried out a running debate over slavery, none were as eloquent as Abraham Lincoln and Stephen Douglas in their famous debates. Neighbors argued with each other, and friends in churches, parlors, and taverns all discussed "the Negro problem." The statements of Lincoln and Douglas expressed the two most widely held opinions in the North.

Lincoln represented the position that slavery was immoral and indefensible for a nation that claimed to be a democracy. It was not possible, he argued, for those who opposed slavery to simply ignore its practice. Ultimately, the entire nation would have to become all free or all slaveholding: "A house divided against itself cannot stand. I believe this government cannot endure permanently half slave and half free. I do not expect this union to be dissolved; I do not expect the house to fall, but I do expect it will cease to be divided. It will become all one thing or all the other."

Douglas countered by asking why the country could not "continue to exist divided into free and slave states." The nation had existed for more than half a century this way. Douglas maintained that the Founding Fathers who wrote the Constitution had "left each state perfectly free to do as it pleased on the subject." To talk of ending this coexistence, he said, was revolutionary and radical. "If the nation cannot endure thus divided, then Lincoln must strive to make them all free or all slave, which will inevitably bring about a dissolution of the Union," Douglas said.

Lincoln knew that Americans at that time would not favor complete abolition of slavery or complete equality for blacks. Whatever he may have believed personally, he did not publicly say that blacks should be given equality. Instead, he proposed nothing more than that slavery should immediately be prohibited from spreading any farther. He stressed that slavery would eventually die in the South as long as it was not condoned elsewhere: "I do not suppose that in the most peaceful way ultimate extinction would occur in less than a hundred years at least, but that it will occur in the best way for both races in God's good time, I have no doubt."

Douglas appealed to white fears and prejudices. "The Negro must always occupy an inferior position," he declared to cheering crowds. "Are you in favor of conferring upon the Negro the rights and privileges of citizenship?" he demanded of his opponent. He warned that Lincoln and his Republicans would free all the Southern slaves, sending "one hundred thousand slaves into Illinois, to become citizens and voters on an equality with yourselves.... If you think that the Negro ought to be on a social equality with your wives and daughters, you have a perfect right to think so.... Those of you who believe that the Negro is your equal, of course will vote for Mr. Lincoln."

Lincoln walked a tightrope on the issue of equality. On occasion, he called on Americans to "discard all this quibbling about this race and that race and the other race being inferior. Let us unite throughout this land, until we shall once more stand up declaring all men are created equal." On other occasions, he qualified considerably what he meant by equality. "In the right to eat the bread, without leave of anybody else, which his own hand earns, the Negro is my equal and the equal of Judge Douglas, and the equal of every living man," Lincoln declared.

In the matter of political equality, however, Lincoln was much more conservative when he said, "I am not, nor ever have been in favor of bringing about in any way the social and political equality of the white and black races. I am not nor ever have been in favor of making voters or jurors of negroes, nor of qualifying them to hold office, nor to intermarry with white people; and I will say in addition to this that there is a physical difference between the races which I believe will forever forbid the two races living together on terms of social and political equality."

his home state of Illinois, and his opponent was Abraham Lincoln. Lincoln was still a little-known figure outside of Illinois, whereas Douglas was among the best-known politicians in the country. Lincoln knew he would have to do something extraordinary to unseat Douglas. So he challenged Douglas to a series of seven debates in different locations throughout the state.

The Lincoln-Douglas debates became the most famous series of political debates in American history. They pitted two masterful orators in a contest of wit, logic, and hard-hitting verbal attacks. They also focused the entire nation's attention on one issue: slavery. With Lincoln taking the antislavery position and Douglas the states' rights position, the sole subject of the seven Lincoln-Douglas debates was slavery. Although Douglas won the 1858 election to the Senate, Lincoln's challenge was nearly successful. More important, the public debates earned him a national reputation as the spokesman for the Republican party's views on slavery and other national issues.

Unmendable Divisions

As another presidential election year approached, tensions mounted over the Fugitive Slave Law, a foiled attempt by radical slavery opponent John Brown to take a federal arsenal and start a slave rebellion, and the rejection of statehood for Kansas. Divisions over the Kansas decision had hopelessly divided the Democratic party. At the party convention in Charleston, South Carolina, Southern delegates Jefferson Davis and William Yancey disrupted the proceedings to give speeches "for an independent Southern Republic." They implored their fellow Southern slaveholders to follow in the footsteps of the Founding Fathers and lead a second revolution. To many Southerners, the right to own slaves was one of the liberties that their forefathers had fought to secure in the American Revolution. "Perhaps even now," said Yancey, "the pen of the historian is nibbed to write the story of the new revolution."

So divisive was the convention that after six days and fifty-seven ballots, the nomination of a presidential candidate was hopelessly deadlocked. The delegates agreed to adjourn and try again six weeks later in Baltimore. In Baltimore, the Northerners managed to put together enough votes to make Stephen Douglas the party nominee. The Southerners were so outraged by this that they walked out of the convention and named their own candidate: John C. Breckinridge of Kentucky. Breckinridge, who was Buchanan's vice president, ran on a platform with one key plank: a slave code legalizing slavery in all U.S. territories.

With the Democrats split, the young Republican party gained the chance to win the presidency and advance its antislavery policy. The party shrewdly nominated Lincoln, regarded by most

Northerners as a moderate who could appeal to many Democrats and former Whigs. He would also be the choice of the abolitionists, for even though he did not represent their position on equality, he was far closer to it than any of the other candidates.

Southerners, however, hated Lincoln. They believed he stood for the total abolition of slavery—perhaps not immediately but eventually. To Southerners, this made him anything but moderate. They believed his election and a strong representation of Republicans in the Senate would be signs of an irreversible trend to end the South's domination of national politics. Southerners were convinced that the election of Lincoln would be the ruin of the South. One local politician said, "Rather than submit to such humiliation and degradation as the inauguration of Abraham Lincoln, we will see Pennsylvania Avenue paved ten fathoms deep with mangled bodies."

Sam Houston, governor of Texas, believed that if the South seceded from the Union a bloody civil war would ensue.

Lincoln's Victory Brings Secession

When election day finally came, on November 6, 1860, Lincoln's name did not even appear on the ballot in ten Southern states. But because the Democratic vote was divided among Douglas, Breckinridge, and a pro-Southern Whig named John Bell, Lincoln won the election. In the South, news of Lincoln's victory raised the cry for secession to a fever pitch. Immediately, the legislature of South Carolina called a special convention to consider seceding from the Union.

Six weeks later, on December 20, 1860, South Carolina voted to secede. On January 9, Mississippi became the second state to secede. The next day, Florida followed. Within the month, Alabama, Georgia, Louisiana, and Texas had all seceded. Sam Houston, the governor of Texas, was against secession, and he warned of the bloody conflict he foresaw:

> Let me tell you what is coming. After the sacrifice of countless millions of treasure and hundreds of thousands of lives, you *may* win Southern independence, but I doubt it. The North is determined to preserve this union. They are not a fiery, impulsive people as you are, for they live in colder climates. But when they begin to move in a given direction, they move with the steady momentum of a mighty avalanche.

Texans voted to secede anyway, and Sam Houston stepped down as governor. On February 8, 1861, delegates from the seven states that had seceded met in Montgomery, Alabama, to form a new nation called the Confederate States of America. They adopted a provisional constitution that was almost identical to the U.S. Constitution, except that it protected the right to own slaves in all states and future territories of the Confederacy.

Jefferson Davis

Abraham Lincoln was not the only American president born in Kentucky in the early 1800s. Jefferson Davis was also born there in 1808, one year before Lincoln. Davis went on to become the only president in the brief history of the Confederate States of America.

Davis's family moved to Mississippi while he was still a child, and he later became a successful planter and slave owner. In 1847, Davis became a Democratic senator from Mississippi, but he resigned after one term to run for governor of the state. He lost, but in 1853, President Franklin Pierce appointed him to his cabinet as the secretary of war.

Davis returned to the Senate in 1857 and carried on the fight for states' rights begun by John C. Calhoun. He remained in the Senate until Mississippi seceded in 1861. On February 18, 1861, he was named the provisional president of the Confederate States of America, and a year later, he was inaugurated as the regular president.

Quite possibly, no other person could have done any better as the president of the Confederacy, but many historians fault Davis for trying to manage the government and the war single-handedly. His opponents criticized him bitterly for mismanaging the war and refusing to accept advice.

Jefferson Davis was sworn in as president of the Confederate States on February 18, 1861. Knowing the difficulties faced by the South's leader, Lincoln often took comfort in saying that "The only person with a job worse than mine must be old Jeff Davis."

The delegates chose Jefferson Davis, one of the South's most prominent statesmen, to be its provisional president. As a former U.S. senator and secretary of war, he was also one of the South's most experienced and able politicians. Although he favored secession, Davis was not as radical as many secessionists. While others called for military action to drive the Yankees out of forts in the South, Davis stressed that the South did not want war with the North; it just wanted to be left alone.

President Lincoln could never accept that position. Before he had even taken the oath of office, he had made restoring the Union his highest priority. Everything else in his platform—resolving the slavery issue, building canals and cross-country railroads, passing tariffs to protect American industry—suddenly became unimportant. The nation he had been elected to lead had been attacked and divided. He now had only one mission: to restore the Union.

The difficult problem for Lincoln was how to restore the Union without causing an all-out war. This was made more difficult by the fact that he did not officially become president until March 4, 1861. By then, the seven slave states of the Deep South had already seceded. Like most Northerners, Lincoln had not expected secession fever to spread so quickly. After all, Southerners had been threatening secession for the past fifty years.

In the past, however, the slave owners had managed to elect a president whom they could influence. They had maintained a strong measure of control over national affairs. Now, everything had changed. Lincoln's election meant that the South had lost much of its national power. Rather than submit to the leadership of Northerners who openly condemned their way of life, Southern slave owners were prepared to fight.

The slave owners also realized that unless a majority of Southern whites supported secession, they could not hope to make their nation last. Therefore, they undertook a campaign to convince the nonslaveholders that they, too, had a stake in the Confederacy. That stake was white supremacy. "The race of white men," declared Georgia governor Joseph Brown, "is the only true aristocracy." As long as blacks were kept as slaves, then all white men were their superiors. Free them from slavery, warned slaveholders, and these black savages would rise up and overrun the poor whites.

Slaveholders created hysteria throughout the South by claiming that the election of Lincoln was part of a Republican scheme to free the blacks and lead them in revolt against the whites. The rich slaveholders would be able to protect themselves, they said. It would be the poor whites who would suffer. A Georgia secessionist warned that if Georgia remained in a Union "ruled by Lincoln and his crew, in TEN years or less our

Abraham Lincoln

Abraham Lincoln was born in a log cabin near Hodgenville, Kentucky, in 1809. He grew up on the frontier in Indiana and Illinois, where he worked splitting logs into fence rails. He never had a formal education, but he was an avid reader. As a young man, he often walked several miles to borrow books, and he taught himself enough law to become a member of the Illinois State Bar.

With his quick wit and animated features, Lincoln was a compelling speaker and entered into state politics. After serving four terms in the Illinois state legislature, he was elected to Congress for one term.

In 1860, he became only the second Republican presidential candidate—and the first to win the presidency, even though he won less than 40 percent of the popular vote. In many Southern states, Lincoln's name did not even appear on the ballot. When he took office in 1861, Lincoln was still not well known in the North, either. Many political experts doubted that this unpolished lawyer from Illinois could handle the shrewd politicians of Washington, D.C.

He soon proved that he was more than fit for the job, even during the most trying days of the nation's history. By the time of his death in 1865, Abraham Lincoln had become, in the eyes of

With Lincoln's election, the secession of the South was inevitable. One Southern newspaper said that it would rather see "Pennsylvania Avenue paved ten fathoms deep with mangled bodies" than submit to an administration headed by Lincoln.

the world, equal in stature to George Washington. Since then, Abraham Lincoln has been considered by many Americans to be the greatest American president in history for his role in preserving the Union and in ending slavery throughout the nation.

The second inauguration of Abraham Lincoln in 1865. Lincoln can be seen on the lower deck at the small, white table.

CHILDREN will be the SLAVES of negroes." A South Carolina preacher contributed to this hysteria with his prediction. "Abolition preachers will be at hand to consummate the marriage of your daughters to black husbands.... Submit to have our wives and daughters choose between death and gratifying the hellish lust of the negro? Better ten thousand deaths than submission to Black Republicanism." To protect their wives and daughters, poor white Southerners joined with slaveholders behind the new Confederate flag.

The Upper South

On March 4, 1861, Lincoln took the oath of office as the sixteenth president of the United States. In his inaugural address, he expressed his desire for peace and reconciliation with the South. "We are not enemies but friends," he said. While swearing to defend the Union and Union property, he promised not to attack the South unless the South attacked first. Furthermore, he repeated his pledge not to abolish slavery in any of the existing slave states and to enforce the Fugitive Slave Law.

Lincoln's appeal for compromise alienated both abolitionists and supporters of slavery. But these people were not the audience Lincoln was trying to reach. Instead, he was aiming his remarks at the citizens of the eight states of the Upper South— Delaware, Maryland, Virginia, North Carolina, Tennessee, Kentucky, Missouri, and Arkansas.

These eight slave states had so far decided not to secede, and Lincoln knew that if they did, the Confederacy's new government might succeed. Two-thirds of the South's total white population lived in these states. In addition, almost the entire industrial capacity of the South and more than half of its livestock and food crops came from this region. With the addition of all eight states of the Upper South, the Confederacy had a good chance of withstanding any Union challenge. But a nation composed only of the original seven states of the Confederacy was just a Southern fantasy.

Lincoln had been able to maintain enough support for the Union in these states to keep them from seceding. One reason for that was his diplomatic handling of cabinet appointments and other attempts to build a workable compromise with Northern Democrats.

Another reason the Upper South was not as anxious to secede was that it had more in common with its Northern neighbors. Only one out of five white families in the Upper South owned slaves, compared with nearly twice that percentage in the Deep South. The states of the Upper South were also more industrial and benefited from the same kinds of tariff laws and transportation development that most Northerners supported.

After Lincoln's inauguration, Maj. Robert Anderson, commander of Fort Sumter, feared a Rebel attack.

(Above) Fort Sumter, South Carolina, as viewed from Charleston Harbor. (Right) The bombardment of Fort Sumter lights up the night sky.

Fort Sumter

On March 5, 1861, one day after taking office, Lincoln received a letter from Maj. Robert Anderson, the commander of Fort Sumter, one of the Union's few manned installations in the South. It was located on an island in Charleston Harbor, off the coast of South Carolina. Anderson urgently requested that Lincoln authorize additional troops for Fort Sumter, in case the Confederates attacked it. Lincoln, however, hesitated to send troops, thinking such an action might spur the Confederates to attack.

Anderson's prediction proved correct. Confederates considered the federal troops at Fort Sumter to be a foreign occupying force, and they demanded that the fort be evacuated and turned over to the Confederacy. By assembling the South Carolina militia and calling for volunteers to join them, the Confederates mustered an army of about six thousand men in Charleston. Jefferson Davis placed Gen. Pierre Beauregard, a graduate of West Point and a veteran of the Mexican War, in command of these troops. Ironically, while at West Point in the 1830s, Beauregard had

The interior of Fort (Left) Sumter after it had been evacuated by Anderson and his men. (Above) Another view of the interior shows some of the devastation wreaked by the Confederate bombardment.

studied under Major Anderson, and the two had become friends. Now, it was his friend Anderson who commanded the troops at Fort Sumter.

Anderson's tiny force of eighty-six men, eight of whom were musicians, was soon surrounded on three sides by Beauregard's six thousand men. On April 12, 1861, at 3:30 A.M., Beauregard sent a messenger to demand Anderson's peaceful surrender. When Anderson refused, Confederate batteries opened fire from every point on the harbor. For thirty-six hours, the small group of soldiers in the fort returned fire. From rooftops or at the waterfront, practically every citizen of Charleston watched the battle from start to finish. Neither side experienced any casualties, but Fort Sumter was ablaze, and it stood in ruins.

At 7:00 P.M. on April 13, Anderson surrendered. He agreed that his men would depart from Fort Sumter the next day. On the morning of April 14, General Beauregard allowed his old friend a one-hundred-gun salute to the tattered Union flag. Thousands watched from boats in the harbor as Old Glory was lowered amid the cannons' roar. A spark from one of the cannons

A view of Fort Sumter shows the damage caused by the Confederate attack. When flame and smoke engulfed the fort, many women spectators wept for its defenders.

P.G.T. Beauregard commanded the Confederate forces that attacked Fort Sumter. A West Point graduate and a Mexican War hero, Beauregard had excellent credentials.

ignited the powder in Union private Daniel Hough's gun. The gun exploded, tearing off the soldier's right arm and killing him instantly. Hough became the first fatality of the Civil War.

As the flag of the new Confederacy flew above Fort Sumter and Beauregard's men tasted the first sweet fruit of victory, Major Anderson tucked the tattered American flag gently under his arm, saluted, and boarded a ship bound for Washington. The bloodiest and most devastating war in American history had begun with so little bloodshed it was almost as if nothing had happened. No war had been declared, no prisoners taken, no enemies killed in battle. But everything had changed. The first angry fire had been exchanged between North and South, and now everyone waited, on both sides, to see what Abraham Lincoln and Jefferson Davis would do next.

CHAPTER THREE

Amateurs at War

News of the surrender at Fort Sumter spread through the country by telegraph, newspaper, and word of mouth. In Union and Confederate states alike, the news set off a wave of patriotism and calls for war. Young Southerners flocked to join the state militias, answering President Jefferson Davis's call for 100,000 volunteers. The Rebel recruits knew they might be outnumbered by the armies of the more heavily populated North, yet most of them fully believed that one Southern boy, taught since childhood to ride and shoot, could whip ten Yankee clerks and shopkeepers.

These volunteers were recruited to serve for three months because no one expected the fighting to last any longer. The people of the South did not think the Yankees would fight very hard just to force a handful of slave states back into the Union. Once the Confederates demonstrated their willingness to fight for their independence, they expected the North to leave them alone.

The Confederates underestimated the depth of patriotism and emotion stirred by the attack on Fort Sumter. Before Fort Sumter, Republicans, abolitionists, and Northern Democrats were bitterly divided over how to react to Southern secession. Afterward, they were united in their desire to restore the Union. President Lincoln said, "This issue embraces more than the fate of these United States. It presents to the whole family of man, the question, whether a constitutional republic, or a democracy can or cannot maintain its territorial integrity against its own domestic foes."

In the name of the flag, the Union, the Constitution, democracy, and "the best government on earth," hundreds of thousands

A battalion of Union soldiers defends the White House in the early years of the Civil War.

of Americans rallied in the streets of Northern cities to support a war that would force the Rebels to renounce their independence. When Lincoln put out a call for seventy-five thousand volunteers to serve for three months defending Washington, D.C., against a possible attack, young men responded with overwhelming enthusiasm.

No Mention of Slavery

Ironically, the one issue that scarcely anyone mentioned was slavery. It became the great unspoken cause of the war. President Lincoln knew that it had not only divided Northerners from Southerners but that Northerners themselves were bitterly divided over the slave issue. He had won less than half of the popular vote in the Union states with his antislavery campaign. He knew that his views did not reflect a majority opinion and that most Yankee soldiers were more willing to die for the Union or for democracy than for the freedom of Southern slaves.

Southern leaders also had a difficult time with the slavery issue. Most Southern soldiers did not own slaves, so their leaders did not state publicly that they were fighting to preserve the institution of slavery. Instead, they were fighting to defend their homeland against Northern invaders and to protect the "sacred rights of liberty and self-government."

While Lincoln's call to arms unified the North solidly behind him, it had the opposite effect on the border states. Virginia and North Carolina were deadlocked on the issue of secession at the time of the Confederate attack on Fort Sumter. On April 15, when Lincoln called for troops from "every loyal Union state," the people in Virginia and North Carolina reacted angrily. They refused to send troops to fight against fellow Southerners. Huge pro-Southern crowds gathered to voice their support for the Confederacy, and in May conventions, both states voted to secede. Shortly thereafter, the Confederate cabinet decided unanimously to move its capital from remote Montgomery, Alabama, to centrally located Richmond, Virginia.

Overzealous secessionists in the Virginia militia did not wait for the state to officially secede. In April, they attacked the weakly defended Union arsenal at Harpers Ferry and seized all the weapons and arms manufacturing equipment there. They shipped this equipment to a small steel mill in Richmond, which became the Confederacy's primary supplier of weapons throughout the war.

Another Virginia militia unit marched on the Gosport Navy Yard on the Elizabeth River near Norfolk, Virginia. Although it was the Union's most important naval station in Virginia, it was not strongly defended. The Union commander at Gosport ordered a full retreat. Rather than give up a single ship, he commanded that every ship that could not immediately be put out to sea should be burned instead.

Only three ships managed to get away. The rest were burned and sank in the river. Unfortunately for the North, the river was so shallow that the burned-out boats were easy to retrieve. In addition to the boats, the militiamen captured about one thousand heavy naval guns, which were used at Confederate fortifications throughout the South. These heroics by the Virginia militia helped make it possible to supply the Confederate army with rifles, artillery, and ammunition throughout the war.

A view of Harpers Ferry, West Virginia, shows the Shenandoah and Potomac rivers. In April 1861, the Virginia military attacked the arsenal at Harpers Ferry and seized weapons and manufacturing equipment.

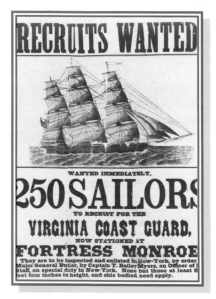

Naval recruitment posters incite young men to defend their country. Young men in both the South and the North responded enthusiastically to the call to arms.

All Hope Gone?

Lincoln still hoped that war could be avoided. "I will not say that all hope is yet gone," he declared. Though reluctant to launch a military invasion of the South, he knew that the Union had to prepare for one. The attack on Fort Sumter had been an act of war, and the Union had to respond.

Jefferson Davis, too, hoped to avoid a full-scale war with the North. He even admitted that "separation is not, of necessity, final." He realized how difficult it would be for the Confederacy to develop economic and military independence. It would need factories, railroads, military weapons and artillery, and an army. It would have to develop a shipping industry to continue selling cotton and tobacco to the Europeans. These things would be hard enough to do without fighting a war at the same time against the North with its established army and navy, its industrial resources, and its larger population.

More than once over the next four years, Lincoln would find comfort by saying, "The only person with a job worse than mine must be old Jeff Davis." Indeed, Lincoln's troubles might have seemed trivial to Davis. The North had approximately 3.5 million able-bodied men between the ages of eighteen and forty-five from whom to recruit soldiers. The South had only about one-third that number. In 1861, the South's only artillery factory was the one that the Virginia militia had dismantled and transported from Harpers Ferry. Its only navy was the Union boats that had been salvaged at Norfolk.

Davis believed that the only way the south could win the war was to adopt a defensive strategy. Rather than attacking the North, the Confederacy could eventually win the war just by holding out against the Union and defending its territory. Knowing the local terrain and having shorter supply and communication lines than the enemy, a Confederate army could quite possibly stop an invasion by a much larger army.

This was probably the most promising strategy for the South, but Davis soon found it impossible to sustain, for political reasons. The temperament of the Southern people prevented any strategy from working that demanded patience. Believing they could whip any number of Yankees, many Rebels scorned the defensive strategy. A columnist for the *Richmond Examiner* wrote, "The idea of waiting for blows, instead of inflicting them, is altogether unsuited to the genius of our people."

Another obstacle facing Davis was that since Southerners were fighting for states' rights, it was extremely difficult to put together a unified national war strategy. Many Southerners, including Col. Robert E. Lee, believed they were fighting to defend their own states more than a Confederate government.

President Lincoln also wanted to play a waiting game. But he, too, had trouble convincing his citizens to be patient. After the Fort Sumter attack, Lincoln continued to look for ways to compromise with the South. In a message to Congress on July 4, 1861, Lincoln reaffirmed that he had "no purpose, directly or indirectly, to interfere with slavery in the States where it exists."

At the start of the Civil War, very few men had battle experience. All volunteers had to be trained in battlefield basics. Here, troops drill at a New York training camp in 1861.

General Scott's Strategy

These limited objectives demanded a strategy for limited warfare, and Union general Winfield Scott provided the perfect plan. Instead of invading the South, he proposed surrounding it with blockades by sea from the east and south and by land and river from the west and north. By sealing the South off from outside supplies, the Union could eventually force it into submission without causing great devastation to the South or a great loss of lives. On April 20, Lincoln implemented the first phase of Scott's plan by ordering a naval blockade of all Southern ports. Although the South used fast-moving clipper sailboats, which they called blockade runners, to sneak goods through the blockade, the supply of foreign imports to the South was drastically reduced. Gradually, this drove the cost of manufactured goods sky-high.

Winfield Scott had picked two men to lead the Union forces: George B. McClellan, a thirty-four-year-old West Pointer who had resigned his army commission to go into the railroad business, and forty-two-year-old Mexican War veteran Maj. Irvin McDowell. Scott promoted both men to the rank of brigadier general. He assigned McClellan to lead Union operations in the Midwest and appointed McDowell to command the army of thirty thousand soldiers now assembled in Washington.

On May 23, 1861, Scott decided to send troops into Virginia to seize and hold a buffer zone in order to defend Washington.

George McClellan

Maj. Gen. George McClellan graduated second in his West Point class and went almost immediately into active duty in the Mexican War, where he served with distinction. In 1857, McClellan resigned from the army and turned to business. There, his considerable organizational skills and demand for perfection soon allowed him to achieve the position of president of the Ohio and Mississippi Railroad.

A Northern Democrat who believed in a state's right to determine its own policy on slavery, McClellan campaigned for Stephen Douglas in the 1860 election. Like Douglas, McClellan was also a loyal unionist, and he reenlisted in the Union army after the fall of Fort Sumter. His first action in the Civil War was as commander of the Army of Ohio. While serving in that capacity, his victories in western Virginia paved the way for that region's 1863 admission to the Union as the new state of West Virginia.

McClellan's first task as Commander of the Army of the Potomac was getting soldiers back on duty. He appointed more than one thousand tough, regular army men to temporary duty as military police. They stormed the local brothels, gambling houses, and saloons, arresting everyone in uniform who could not show written authorization to be away from his post. Within two weeks, almost all soldiers were either back on duty or in the guardhouse, the military jail.

Next, McClellan turned his attention to training the soldiers. Drilling them in all the rudiments of marching and appropriate military demeanor, he fashioned them into a first-class, well-disciplined, well-drilled army. At least once a week, he put his army on parade in a grand review. The army would march smartly in formation, and for a finale, McClellan would invariably come galloping down the ranks on his magnificent war-horse, Dan Webster.

Maj. Gen. George McClellan consistently over-estimated the strength of enemy troops.

The people of Washington, D.C., were relieved they had a first-rate army nearby to defend them. By October, Lincoln and General Scott were anxious to send their new Army of the Potomac into action. From his scouting reports, however, McClellan estimated that the enemy had positioned an enormous army of "not less than 150,000" in Centreville. So McClellan set his sights on a more lightly defended Confederate position at Leesburg, Virginia, thirty-five miles up the Potomac from Washington. This was the first inkling Lincoln had of McClellan's major flaws. McClellan constantly underestimated his own troop strength and overestimated his enemy's. He also revealed a contempt for Lincoln, once describing him as "the original gorilla."

Led by General McDowell, the operation went smoothly. With surprisingly little bloodshed, the Union army established its buffer zone on the Virginia side of the Potomac River. Only one soldier, a Union officer, was killed. The Union established a toe-hold on Virginia's eastern seaboard by taking Fort Monroe at the mouth of Chesapeake Bay, about sixty miles south of Richmond. General Scott knew his fellow Virginians well enough to know that every one of those sixty miles would be fiercely defended. He chose to continue his policy of limited confrontation.

There was only one problem. The Union commander at Fort Monroe, Benjamin Butler, wanted glory. Without Scott's approval, Butler, who had no previous battle experience, set out from Fort Monroe with forty-four hundred freshly recruited, unseasoned troops to march on Richmond. On the morning of June 10, they were met and forced back to Fort Monroe by Confederate troops at a railroad junction called Big Bethel. On the war's first battlefield, eighteen Yankee soldiers died and more than fifty others were wounded. No one was prepared to witness such destruction. Even the Confederates, who suffered only light casualties, were appalled. When he surveyed the battlefield, Confederate lieutenant Benjamin Huske cried out, "Great God in mercy, avert the awful results of civil war!"

But the battle at Big Bethel meant that war could no longer be averted. The North had attacked the Confederacy, and neither Lincoln nor Davis could do anything to stop the awful march toward war. A major clash was inevitable.

Maj. Gen. Irvin McDowell commanded the Union troops in Washington.

Bull Run

The first major confrontation of the Civil War finally came on a hot July day beside a little Virginia stream called Bull Run. The battle that took place there is known as the First Battle of Bull Run. The prize of this battle was control of the town called Manassas Junction, a strategic railroad junction about thirty miles southwest of Washington. Here, trains carried Rebel troops to reinforce the Confederacy's northern defenses. Here, too, the Manassas Gap Railroad headed west into the Shenandoah Valley. This beautiful Virginia valley was not only a vital agricultural area but a strategic location from which the Rebels could launch a campaign against Washington. If it fell into Yankee hands, the valley would be an ideal invasion route into the heart of Virginia.

Determined to hold Manassas Junction, Jefferson Davis sent the flamboyant General Beauregard, hero of Fort Sumter, to defend it. Beauregard chose the tall, densely wooded banks of Bull Run as the best natural barrier against attack. Only one bridge across the stream, at Warrenton Turnpike, could support the heavy wagon traffic of an invading army. And there were only a few places where the brush was clear enough to allow an

Disastrous Strategies

The North had far more artillery than the South but not any guns that were more powerful or more accurate. The rifles developed in the 1850s and 1860s could be loaded much faster and were more accurate than anything used in combat before. These weapons turned the traditional open battlefield, in which one side stood its ground while the other marched toward it in rank and file, into a deadly killing field.

When the Civil War began, many infantrymen, especially on the Confederate side, were still using muskets, which fired round balls. After each shot, the soldier had to stop, load a new ball, pour gunpowder into the chamber, and pack it tight with a rod. Soon, muskets were replaced by rifles, which fired cone-shaped bullets. The powder in these guns was packed in a separate cartridge. With the introduction of the Colt and lever-action Spencer repeating rifles midway through the war, sol-diers could fire even faster. These rifles were the first to use bullets with the powder cartridge already attached, and they contained a magazine, or a cylinder, that allowed the soldier to fire between five and seven times before having to reload.

In a war that most people expected to last only weeks, most Civil War generals did not learn to alter their strategies to accommodate these improvements in weaponry. The result was the bloodiest war ever engaged in by Americans. In previous wars, troops marched in straight rows and made orderly offensive charges in row upon row. It was an effective strategy, too, because of the time it took the defensive soldiers to load and reshoot. In that time, a high percentage of charging soldiers had a chance to break through enemy lines and engage in hand-to-hand combat. The loser in a hand-to-hand fight was seldom killed. More often, he was wounded and taken prisoner.

In this illustration, Civil War battle strategy can be clearly seen. Battalions of troops march headlong into each other's fire. Because of newly developed weaponry, this strategy resulted in enormous casualties.

The introduction of repeating rifles changed warfare dramatically. The ability of soldiers to fire many more shots without reloading resulted in an incredibly high number of casualties. Pictured here are details of the Spencer repeating rifle. Seven cartridges fit into a tubelike magazine, which was inserted through the butt. When the soldier depressed the loading lever, a spring in the magazine fed a bullet into the breech mechanism. Then, as the soldier raised the lever, the bullet passed into the firing chamber. After firing, the breech mechanism also extracted the spent case each time it was reloaded. The men in the photograph hold another type of repeating rifle, the Colt revolving rifle. These rifles were equipped with a five-shot cylinder.

In the Civil War, generals still sent their troops charging into enemy fire in straight rows. But the defending army could load, aim, and refire so much more quickly than in the past that this strategy cost thousands more lives. The number of troops facing each other was also many times greater than anything American soldiers had known before. Thousands of soldiers would march toward a regiment dug in along a roadway, a wall, or a stream. As the enemy opened fire, the rows of charging soldiers would fall like gigantic dominoes in the field. As they drew closer, the firing continued at point-blank range. The smoke was usually so heavy that the soldiers could barely make out the shapes of the men surrounding them.

Union troops clash with Rebel soldiers in the First Battle of Bull Run.

army to cross the stream. In these areas and near Warrenton Turnpike is where Beauregard positioned his troops.

On July 16, a hot, muggy day in the nation's capital, Union general Irvin McDowell gave orders for an army of thirty-five thousand men, the largest force ever gathered in North America, to set out for Fairfax Court House, a few miles south of Washington. They found no Rebel forces waiting for them there, and so McDowell made plans to press on to Manassas Junction.

The first Union column to reach Bull Run was commanded by Brig. Gen. Daniel Tyler. Although Tyler had been instructed not to fight, he became convinced that his brigade, along with that of Col. Israel Richardson, could cross the stream at a shallow area called Blackburn's Ford and draw the Rebels into battle. What Tyler did not see was that three full brigades of enemy troops were already hiding in the brush along the stream's south bank, with another brigade in reserve behind them.

When the first Union troops reached the stream, the Confederates stood and opened fire. Tyler sent several more units toward the ford before he realized the strength of the Confederate resistance and the folly of his attack. Then, he ordered a full retreat.

When General McDowell heard the report of this skirmish, he was furious. Pulling Union troops back to the town of Centreville, McDowell had to make a new plan. July 21 was set for a second attempt at taking Manassas Junction. This time, McDowell planned to cross Bull Run farther north at Sudley Ford.

Beauregard, however, was convinced that the tangle of roads through the brush at Sudley Ford was too confusing for McDowell to even attempt a crossing. So, he deployed no troops there. Fortunately for the Rebels, word had reached Gen. Joseph Johnston in the Shenandoah Valley that Beauregard might need reinforcements. While Union leader McDowell waited at Centreville for wagonloads of fresh supplies, Johnston loaded his ten thousand men on the Manassas Gap Railroad and headed for Manassas Junction. He arrived on July 20, before McDowell's second attack.

Picnics at the Battle Site

Johnston's men were not the only ones to crowd into Manassas Junction. Thousands of civilians from Washington and the surrounding countryside had gathered to watch the coming battle. They came with their picnic baskets and their blankets, and they drove their wagons to choice positions on high ground where they could see what was happening on the battlefields below.

On the morning of July 21, McDowell's men marched on Bull Run again. This time, Tyler obeyed orders and feigned an attack at the Warrenton Turnpike Bridge. In charge of the Rebel brigade stationed at the bridge was Col. Nathan Evans, a gruff soldier from South Carolina who loved a good fight.

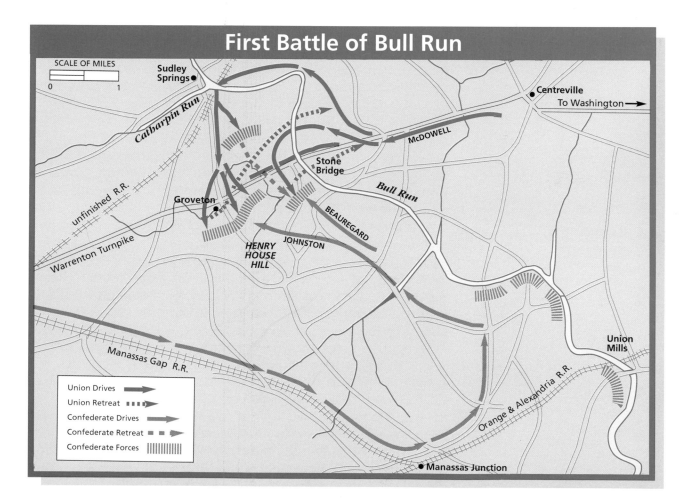

*Confederate general Joseph John-
ston loaded his ten thousand
men on the Manassas Gap Railroad and arrived in Manassas
Junction in time to reinforce
Beauregard's troops.*

Evans was nearly fooled by Tyler's diversion, but just as he was about to direct his men toward Tyler, one of his soldiers, perched high above the trees on a signal tower, spotted bayonets glinting in the sun farther to the north. Quickly, he sent a message to Evans: "Look out on your left, you are turned."

Leaving four companies to face Tyler at the bridge, Evans took the rest of his brigade and hurried north to cut off the flank of Union soldiers heading for Sudley Ford. The Rebels were greatly outnumbered, and it would not have been surprising to see them retreat.

Instead, a battalion of five hundred fighters who called themselves the Louisiana Tigers led the Rebel charge down a hill toward the more powerful Yankee force. As they charged, the Rebels screamed a wild, high-pitched yell. This threw the Yankee soldiers into such confusion that they retreated before the much smaller Confederate force. The chilling, frenzied screaming by thousands of charging soldiers had been the Rebels' most effective weapon. More than once during the coming years of battle, the "Rebel yell" confused and demoralized a stronger Yankee force and helped gain Rebel victories.

Yet no amount of yelling could stem the tide of Yankee reinforcements forever. Just as the Confederates were preparing to retreat to a new defensive position along the Warrenton Turnpike, a regiment of gray-uniformed men appeared from that direction. Rejoicing, the Confederates thought they had been saved by replacements from the rear.

It was a fatal mistake. Once within rifle range, the newcomers unleashed a murderous volley of gunfire. They were not Rebel replacements at all. The gray-uniformed Second Wisconsin Battalion, from Tyler's brigade, was now pouring it on the Confederates. Surrounded by Yankees, Evans's troops scattered. Just then, General McDowell rode up and shouted, "Victory! Victory! The day is ours!" His elation, however, was premature.

The largest part of the Confederate forces had been situated about five miles to the south at Blackburn's Ford, where Beauregard was convinced the real Yankee attack would take place. Finally, General Johnston, who had brought his troops from the Shenandoah Valley to support Beauregard, grew impatient. "The battle is there," he cried. "I am going."

By the time Johnston arrived at the scene of the battle, the Rebels had retreated south of Bull Run and were struggling to hold off the Yankees near the crest of Henry House Hill. Following Johnston's brigade was another Shenandoah brigade commanded by Gen. Thomas J. Jackson. Brig. Gen. Barnard Bee, who was among the retreating Rebels, turned just in time to see Jackson's Virginians holding firm at the end of the hill. Rallying his men, Bee shouted, "There stands Jackson like a stone wall! Rally behind the Virginians!" Bee, who was mortally wounded later in the day, gave Jackson his nickname, "Stonewall."

By two in the afternoon, Beauregard finally arrived at Henry House Hill as well, bringing the total of Confederate troops there to about sixty-five hundred. The Yankee force massing before them, however, had risen to more than eleven thousand men. For the next two hours, the two armies surged forward and back. Then, Stonewall Jackson made his move. His regiment swept over the hill and captured the Union guns. They were followed by the Fifth Virginia Regiment led by General Beauregard himself. "Give them the bayonet! Give it to them freely!" cried the Confederate general.

Finally, the Union line began to weaken and hesitate. Beauregard, sensing the decisive moment, led his entire line in attack, and the Yankee front simply collapsed. By 4:30 P.M., McDowell recalled, "The entire plain was covered with retreating troops. The retreat soon became a riot, and this soon degenerated still further into a panic." Defeated, the Union army stumbled and lurched back to Washington.

Newspapers throughout the South heralded the Confederate victory in the first great battle of the Civil War. It had been a surprisingly vicious first battle. The Confederates counted nearly four hundred killed, sixteen hundred wounded, and thirteen missing. The North's losses were far worse: nearly five hundred dead, one thousand wounded, and almost two thousand either captured or presumed dead.

In the North, everyone wondered what had gone wrong. Union soldiers had greatly outnumbered their Rebel opposition, yet they had been defeated. One reason for this was that the Civil War was fought mostly by amateurs but with weapons that were capable of far greater destruction than those used in any previous war. Many of the men appointed as generals on both sides had little or no war experience. Regiments were formed locally, and the men appointed to lead them were often chosen by popular vote of the troops themselves or by state political leaders. Few officers on either side knew very much about strategy or about the kind of rigid discipline required to keep a company of soldiers together under heavy fire.

Bull Run was the first battle to bring some of these realities to the country's attention. Spectators had driven their carriages out to Manassas Junction hoping to see an exciting and glorious battle. They, like the soldiers, were not prepared for the gory spectacle. When the battle ended, both sides withdrew in shock and horror at what had taken place. Wounded and dead soldiers and bodies without limbs or heads were strewn across the battlefield. The Confederates, although they had been victorious, were too appalled to pursue the fleeing Yankees.

Stonewall Jackson

Gen. Thomas Jonathan Jackson earned his nickname at Bull Run, but it was his campaign in the Shenandoah Valley of Virginia that would win him undying fame. Anyone who knew Thomas Jackson away from the battlefield would have considered him the most unlikely of heroes. This small, unassuming man wore a faded old uniform left over from the Mexican War era. The visor of his simple soldier's cap shadowed a grim, bearded face. His only outstanding physical features were his size-fourteen feet.

Before the war, Jackson had been a rather boring professor at the Virginia Military Institute. He was a gentle husband and a devoutly religious man who spent hours in prayer each day. He was also a lifelong hypochondriac, always seeking relief for his ailments in peculiar foods and medicines.

But when Jackson stepped onto the field of battle, a transformation occurred. The dreary professor turned into an inspiring commander. His kind, blue eyes burned with a feverish glitter. This gentle, pious man became a pitiless disciplinarian. According to one of his soldiers, "He would have a man shot at the drop of a hat, and drop it himself."

Following the Battle of Bull Run, Jackson's duty became the defense of the Shenandoah Valley. This fertile valley filled with peaceful farms and tobacco plantations was a natural route for invading Virginia. As Jackson once said, "If this valley is lost, Virginia is lost." By the same token, as long as it remained in Rebel control, it was a natural route for invading Washington, D.C.

That made Abraham Lincoln extremely nervous. For more than seven weeks, from mid-April to early June 1862, Jackson's army of

One of the most well-known Confederate generals, Stonewall Jackson was a pious man and a pitiless disciplinarian.

seventeen thousand men gave the Union army fits. They marched more than six hundred miles, twice crossing the entire length of the valley, leading Union forces on a wild-goose chase and evading Yankee efforts to trap them. They launched major attacks on Union encampments five times and on several other occasions achieved small but successful raids.

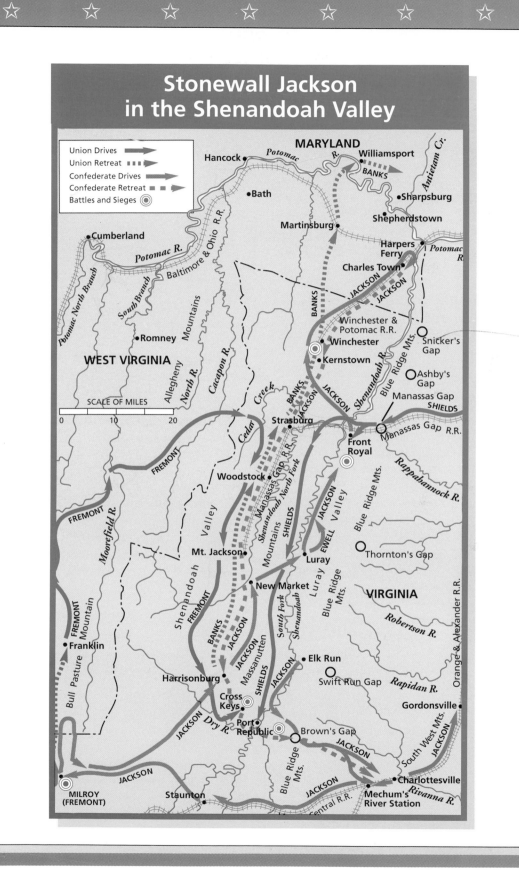

Stonewall Jackson in the Shenandoah Valley

Union Drives
Union Retreat
Confederate Drives
Confederate Retreat
Battles and Sieges

MARYLAND

Hancock
Bath
Cumberland
Martinsburg
Williamsport
Sharpsburg
Shepherdstown
Harpers Ferry
Charles Town

Potomac R.

Antietam Cr.

BANKS

Baltimore & Ohio R.R.

Potomac R.

Potomac North Branch

South Branch

Romney

WEST VIRGINIA

Allegheny Mountains

North R.

Cacapon R.

Cedar Creek

BANKS

JACKSON

JACKSON

Winchester & Potomac R.R.

Winchester
Kernstown

Snicker's Gap

Ashby's Gap

Manassas Gap

SHIELDS

SCALE OF MILES

0   10   20

FREMONT

Strasburg

BANKS
JACKSON

JACKSON

Front Royal

Manassas Gap R.R.

Shenandoah R.

Blue Ridge Mts.

Rappahannock R.

Woodstock

Manassas Gap R.R.

Shenandoah North Fork

SHIELDS

JACKSON

EWELL
Valley

Thornton's Gap

Moorefield R.

FREMONT

Valley

Mt. Jackson

New Market

SHIELDS

Luray

Luray Valley

Blue Ridge Mts.

VIRGINIA

Robertson R.

FREMONT Mountain

Franklin

Bull Pasture

Shenandoah Valley

FREMONT

BANKS

JACKSON

Massanutten

SHIELDS

South Fork Shenandoah

JACKSON

Elk Run

Swift Run Gap

Rapidan R.

Orange & Alexander R.R.

Gordonsville

Harrisonburg

JACKSON

Dry R.

Cross Keys

Port Republic

Brown's Gap

JACKSON

South West Mts.

JACKSON

JACKSON

Blue Ridge Mts.

JACKSON

Charlottesville

Rivanna R.

MILROY (FREMONT)

JACKSON

Staunton

Mechum's River Station

Central R.R.

The success of George McClellan's incessant drilling shows in this photograph of the Army of the Potomac. All during the fall and winter of 1861 McClellan shaped the raw and dispirited troops into an effective fighting force.

In Washington, the army was in a state of disarray. Drunk and demoralized soldiers filled the saloons, and the citizens of Washington worried that if the Rebels, now encamped just twenty-five miles southwest of their city, attacked the capital now, there would be no one to defend it. Lincoln knew that something had to change.

George McClellan

Late in the afternoon on July 16, 1861, five days after the Union's loss at Bull Run, Maj. Gen. George B. McClellan arrived in Washington. Having a reputation for being able to build a highly trained and disciplined army, McClellan had been summoned by Lincoln to assume command of all troops in and about Washington.

Through constant drilling, McClellan was able to take the disorganized Washington troops, now named the Army of the Potomac, and fashion them into a well-disciplined, well-drilled army.

On October 20, after three months of training, McClellan sent two regiments, about two thousand of his fifty thousand men,

The Order of Battle

Battle strategy evolved slowly during the Civil War. At the outset, most strategy was based on the Napoleonic Wars fought half a century earlier in Europe. The side making the attack would march in long rows toward the enemy's defensive position. Although most of the troops were massed in the center, the key to victory was often on the edges, or flanks, of a line. The attacking army would usually attempt some kind of maneuver to outflank, or get around, the outside of the defensive line. With this accomplished, the enemy would be "turned" and forced to fend off attackers from two or more directions at once.

The typical battle units were the cavalry, pickets and skirmishers, infantrymen, and artillery battalions. The cavalry contained troops mounted on horses. They were sometimes used to lead an offensive charge, but more often they were used as scouts to assess enemy positions. Pickets and skirmishers were groups of soldiers also used as scouts. If the company was holding a defensive line, pickets were placed a mile or so in advance of the rest of the company. They would be the first to detect the enemy's advances. An advancing company usually sent skirmishers out ahead into the no-man's-land between the two opposing sides to determine how close the enemy was and which way the troops were lined up. Although battles often began with an exchange of fire between pickets and skirmishers, just as often these soldiers from opposing sides talked to each other, shared the latest news, and even traded rations, tobacco, or coffee before the battle.

The main battle involved the infantry, or the soldiers on foot, and the artillery, which operated the cannons and other large weapons. Typically, the artillery stayed behind the infantry, firing cannonballs and shells over the infantrymen's heads at the enemy. A company on the offensive, advancing on the enemy, usually opened fire with its artillery first to weaken the enemy's defenses before marching the infantry foward.

The Union army opens fire on Rebel troops with its artillery before the infantry advances.

Union troops sustained a devastating loss in the Battle of Ball's Bluff in Virginia. Nearly one thousand soldiers were killed or wounded when they were surprised by Confederate troops.

into action for the first time. The soldiers, all in blue uniforms, marched in step to the rhythm of drums and fifes. They looked like a far more disciplined and confident unit than the random collection of soldiers who had scrambled back to Washington from Bull Run.

The results of this mission were no more encouraging, however. Surprised by Confederates at a hill known as Ball's Bluff, nearly half of the two thousand Yankee soldiers were killed or wounded. About one hundred of them drowned while trying to retreat back across the Potomac River. Although disappointed, General McClellan refused to take the blame for this loss. When he was criticized by General Scott, McClellan complained to Lincoln that it was Scott's interference that prevented him from taking decisive action.

Lincoln had relied on the experience of Winfield Scott and had come to trust his judgment. It was becoming clear, however, that Scott and McClellan could not work together. Furthermore, General Scott was in no physical condition to actually lead the troops, so Lincoln asked him to resign. McClellan became the general in chief of all Union armies.

After the disaster at Ball's Bluff, McClellan put his well-disciplined army through more drills and more parade routines. For weeks, he was contented to keep them in Washington, waiting for the Confederates to make the next move. Members of Congress, the press, and even Lincoln's own cabinet began to wonder openly about McClellan's strategy.

During November, McClellan complained that the weather was unsuitable for a siege of Richmond and that it would have to wait until the following spring. In mid-December, he was stricken with typhoid fever and was unable to leave his bed.

While McClellan was ill, Lincoln appointed a seven-member joint congressional committee to examine issues involving the conduct of the war. The committee became a powerful voice in the nation's affairs, and its chairman, Sen. Benjamin Franklin Wade of Ohio, called loudly for McClellan's dismissal.

Lincoln Borrows the Army

As the year drew to a close and the pressure to act mounted, Lincoln's doubts about his general in chief continued to grow. On January 10, 1862, with McClellan still too ill to lead the army, the president summoned two of McClellan's division commanders to the White House. "If General McClellan does not want to use the Army, I would like to borrow it," chided Lincoln, "provided I could see how it could be made to do something."

Three days later, the president called another meeting at the White House. This time it was to dismiss his secretary of war, Simon Cameron, and appoint Edwin Stanton, an Ohio Democrat, to replace him. Once he assumed his new office, Stanton vowed publicly that he would "force this man McClellan to fight."

Edwin Stanton replaced Simon Cameron as secretary of war in 1862. Frustrated by McClellan's reluctance to use the Army of the Potomac, Stanton vowed that he would force McClellan to fight.

CHAPTER FOUR

The Western Road to Shiloh

While Lincoln and his new secretary of war, Edwin Stanton, anxiously awaited action from the Army of the Potomac, they were also concerned about how the Union's overall plan, as laid out by General Scott, was being followed. That plan called for the Union to press in on the Confederacy from all sides. Just as critical as progress in Virginia was the Union's invasion into the western half of the Confederacy.

The commander in the West was Gen. Henry Halleck. Halleck realized that the key to controlling the West was controlling the Mississippi River. The entire western half of the Confederacy relied on this great river to transport its farm products to New Orleans, the South's most important port. Almost all manufactured products imported into the western states came through New Orleans and up the Mississippi.

Farther north, steamboats on the Tennessee and Cumberland rivers linked Tennessee and northern Alabama to the Mississippi transportation system. During the Civil War, the Confederates used these waterways to ship weapons, ammunition, and even food supplies to their soldiers. Railroads also crossed the western Confederate states, but they did not handle half as much freight as what went up and down these rivers. To gain control of the Tennessee and Cumberland rivers, Halleck called on a scruffy little brigadier general named Ulysses S. Grant.

Victories in the West

The Southern commander in the West was Gen. Albert Sidney Johnston, a tall, handsome man who was admired by both sides.

Western commander Gen. Henry Halleck believed the key to controlling the West was for the Union to control the Mississippi River.

Union general William Tecumseh Sherman called him "a real general, the most formidable man that the Confederacy would produce."

Immediately, Johnston recognized the key weakness of the Confederate western defense was that the forces were too spread out. He decided to concentrate his defense, with about seventy thousand Rebel soldiers, along the northern border of Tennessee, the northernmost Southern state. He stationed his troops at two strong fortifications: Fort Henry on the Tennessee River and, about twelve miles to the east, Fort Donelson on the Cumberland River.

In January 1862, General Grant made his plans to occupy these two forts. To take these forts, Grant needed to attack from the river and from the land simultaneously. Thanks to the foresight of Winfield Scott, the Union had built a fleet of seven ironclad gunboats for just this kind of campaign. In January 1862, the gunboats were ready for service, and General Grant was ready to put them into action.

On February 2, at Paducah, Kentucky, Grant loaded seventeen thousand men onto steamboats and started up the Tennessee River toward Fort Henry, escorted by the seven gunboats under the command of Capt. Andrew Foote. The river was swollen from winter rains and runoff, and it was about to flood the fort. The Confederate commander of Fort Henry was as worried about the rising river as he was about the presence of the Union boats steaming along it. Before the flotilla arrived, he had already sent most of his men to safety at Fort Donelson.

Capt. Andrew Foote commanded the seven gunboats that attacked Fort Henry in Kentucky.

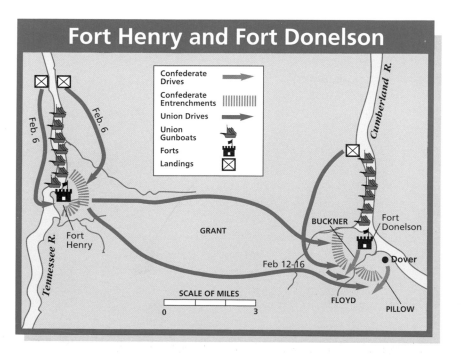

Fort Henry and Fort Donelson

The *Monitor* and the *Merrimac*

The Confederacy possessed only a few warships, but one of them, the *Virginia,* gave the Union a real scare in the spring of 1862. The *Virginia* was the first ironclad warship in the world to go into battle. The hull of this boat was taken from the *Merrimac,* the abandoned Union warship that had been sunk in the harbor at Norfolk, Virginia, to keep it from falling into Confederate hands.

The Confederates were able to retrieve the *Merrimac* from the harbor, and with fifteen hundred men working furiously for ten months, they turned the wooden steamer into a huge, powerful iron warship. On March 8, 1862, the *Virginia* went into battle for the first time, completely demolishing two wooden Union warships. Northerners were startled and deeply alarmed. Southerners were ecstatic. Some Southern newspapers predicted that this one Confederate ship could destroy the whole Union navy.

The Southern euphoria lasted for one day. Secretly, the Union had built its own ironclad warship, the *Monitor,* and on March 9, it sailed south to meet the iron monster from Virginia. The *Monitor* was an even more advanced ship than the *Virginia.* Its huge guns were positioned on a revolving turret that could spin 360 degrees and fire in any direction in minutes. The *Virginia,* on the other hand, had to turn in the water so that its guns, located on the sides, were pointed in the right direction. The *Monitor* was also smaller and quicker than the *Virginia.*

Despite these advantages, the *Monitor* battled the *Virginia* for four hours off the coast at Hampton Roads, Virginia, and did not inflict any damage. The battle of the two iron monsters, which thousands of people watched from shore, was a draw. Not a single sailor on either ship was hurt, and the heavy cannonballs that were fired did little more than dent the iron ships.

As it turned out, neither the *Monitor* nor the *Virginia* saw much action in the Civil War. About two months after their historic battle, Union forces captured Norfolk, where the *Virginia* was stationed. The crew blew up the ship so that it would not fall into Northern hands. Eight months later, the *Monitor* sank in a storm off the coast of North Carolina.

The most lasting influence of the *Monitor* and the *Virginia* (or the *Merrimac*) was that they brought an end to the era of the wooden warship. Never again would a nation build a wooden navy. By the end of the Civil War, the North had already built thirty-one more ironclad gunboats like the *Monitor.*

The first battle between the new ironclad ships took place between the Virginia *and the* Monitor, *pictured here. Ironclads were much more durable and resistant to fire than wooden warships.*

Union soldiers triumph in the capture of Fort Donelson. Ironically, if the Confederates had stuck to their original plan to stay in the fort and withstand Grant's attack they would have been successful. Instead, the Confederates tried to escape the fort and were defeated by Union soldiers.

Still, heavy artillery fire from Fort Henry damaged two of the seven gunboats before they were able to knock out the fort's heaviest guns with their own artillery fire, forcing the Confederates to surrender.

Grant knew that he would meet much heavier resistance at Fort Donelson. Johnston had sent reinforcements to Fort Donelson under three separate generals. On February 12, while Captain Foote directed his fleet of gunboats up the Cumberland River toward the fort, Grant took fifteen thousand troops and marched overland from Fort Henry to Fort Donelson. Expecting that the gunboats would destroy the fort's waterside artillery batteries, Grant positioned his troops south of the fort, blocking the road that the Confederates might try to use to escape.

The attack from the gunboats did not go exactly as planned. They were unable to do much damage to the fort from long range, so Captain Foote ordered the boats to move in and pound the fort from close range. The same tactic had been successful at Fort Henry. But Fort Donelson's artillery power was much greater. It shredded the Union's gunboats, blowing up paddle wheels and blasting holes in the iron hulls. Soon, the Union boats drifted helplessly away.

The fort seemed well prepared to withstand Grant's attack. The three commanders in the fort, however, had been convinced that the Union gunboats would knock out their artillery, leaving them trapped inside. Even though that did not happen, the three commanders still ordered their men to try to escape from the fort. At first, the Confederates managed to push the surprised Yankees back, but Grant kept his calm. He quickly realized that the enemy was trying to escape. He told an aide, "The one who attacks first now will be victorious."

Camp Life

The fighting men of the North and South made the best of life in camp, finding what comfort and enjoyment they could amid the hardships. In spring and summer, when troops were on the move, they slept in canvas tents, often so crowded that when one man rolled over, all the rest had to follow. In autumn, they began to build crude log huts for their winter quarters.

When they were not drilling or standing guard, the troops read, played cards, wrote letters, or sang songs. Almost every company had a drummer, a fife player, and a few banjo or guitar pickers. They improvised well at cutting one another's hair and beards, and most soldiers carried sewing kits to mend their uniforms.

On the night before the battle at Chancellorsville, Virginia, in the summer of 1862, a Confederate soldier wrote to his family that most of his comrades spent the evening sewing their names on their uniforms. That day, they had marched over the unidentified remains of soldiers who had died at the Battle of the Wilderness a year earlier. If they were to fall in battle, too, at least someone would be able to identify them.

This scene greeted Confederate and Union soldiers awaiting the start of the Second Battle of the Wilderness. As soldiers tried to sleep before the next day's battle, these skulls and remains of soldiers from the first battle must have haunted their dreams.

Two pictures of soldiers in permanent winter quarters. Life on the field was far less comfortable. Soldiers were required to perform all their own domestic duties.

Ordering his division commanders to advance and retake lost ground, Grant galloped down the line, shouting, "Fill your cartridge boxes, quick, and get into line. The enemy is trying to escape and he must not be permitted to do so."

Later, Grant recalled, "This acted like a charm. The men only wanted someone to give them a command." As the Union was reclaiming its ground, the Confederate command was disintegrating. Forced to surrender Fort Donelson, the Confederates now had to retreat south, also abandoning Nashville, the capital of Tennessee. It was the first Confederate state capital to be captured by the Union.

Corinth, Mississippi

After its losses in Tennessee, the Confederate army had to establish a new line of defense farther south. General Johnston chose to dig in at Corinth, Mississippi, just south of the Tennessee border and a few miles west of the Tennessee River. Corinth was an important railroad junction where thousands of fresh Confederate troops could easily be transported. They were soon pouring in from every direction, until Johnston had forty thousand men under him. Johnston believed that the time had come to drive the Yankees back, at least into Tennessee and perhaps farther.

On the Union side, Grant also had about forty thousand men, and he urged an immediate attack on Corinth, hoping to catch Johnston by surprise. General Halleck restrained Grant, ordering him to wait until Gen. Don Carlos Buell's Army of the Ohio could join him, adding fifty-five thousand troops to the Union force. So Grant set up his headquarters at Savannah, Tennessee, nine miles from the tiny Tennessee River hamlet of Pittsburg Landing, just north of the Tennessee-Mississippi border. In charge of all regiments under him, Grant placed William Tecumseh Sherman.

Sherman chose a peaceful spot about five miles west of Pittsburg Landing to establish camp. There was nothing there but a crossroads, with a road leading to Corinth, and a small log church. The place was called Shiloh, a biblical name meaning "place of peace." With dogwood trees just starting to blossom in late March of 1862, Shiloh did not seem like the place for a great battle. Actually, neither Grant nor Sherman was expecting a battle to take place there. They did not even order trenches or dirt barricades to be dug.

On April 2, the Confederate commanders at Corinth received a report that Buell was on his way from Nashville with a huge army to join forces with Grant. "Now is the moment to strike the enemy at Pittsburg Landing," wrote Beauregard, General Johnston's second in command. Johnston agreed and instructed him to devise a plan of attack. Beauregard spent the night concocting

Don Carlos Buell, commander of the Army of the Ohio in the Shiloh campaign.

a complex strategy for marching on Shiloh and attacking in three successive waves. It was a plan that called for precise coordination among the various units assembled.

Doomed to Fail

Beauregard's plan was doomed before any battle could occur. First, on the morning of April 3, Gen. William Hardee refused to march without receiving written orders from Johnston. He did not receive the orders until that afternoon, so the attack had to be postponed until April 5. On Saturday, April 5, the troops set out and marched to within two miles of Shiloh. Then a torrential rain turned the roads to mud, and the troops could not march any farther. Beauregard halted their march for the night.

The next morning, Beauregard was sure that his army had made so much noise that they would never surprise the Yankees. Rather than risk marching into a trap, Beauregard called off the attack and ordered the troops to return to Corinth. When Johnston saw them returning, he lost his patience. "This is not war!" he raged.

Beauregard had been right about being detected, though, and he argued that the attack should be called off. Earlier that morning, a Union scout had seen a great sprawl of Confederate camp fires near Shiloh and had informed his brigade commander, Col. Everett Peabody. Peabody sent out a three-hundred-man force that encountered skirmishers, or advance scouts, from one of General Hardee's regiments east of Shiloh at dawn. The two sides exchanged fire.

At Johnston's temporary headquarters on the Corinth Road, Johnston and Beauregard were still arguing about carrying out the attack when Johnston heard the sound of gunfire. Beauregard still wanted to call off the attack, but Johnston cocked his head toward the sound of the guns. "The battle has opened, gentlemen; it is too late to change our dispositions now," he said.

And so the battle that came to be known as "bloody Shiloh" began. Johnston instructed Beauregard to stay in the rear and direct men and supplies to the front while he rode forward to lead the men on the battle line. Before riding to the front, Johnston sent a telegraph to President Davis outlining his plan of attack. The telegraph read: "Polk the left, Bragg the center, Hardee the right, Breckinridge in reserve."

Apparently, Johnston did not communicate his plan to Beauregard, who simply wanted to attack the enemy head on and push them straight eastward into the Tennessee River. Johnston rode off in high spirits. "Tonight," he declared, "we will water our horses in the Tennessee River." As he led his men toward Shiloh, a brilliant, sunny, Sunday morning was dawning over the little church in the Tennessee countryside.

Union colonel Jesse Appler, commander of the Fifty-third Ohio Regiment, was the first to see Confederate movement. Appler's unit was positioned on the extreme west end of the Union line. The Confederates marched forward, row after row, into Appler's waiting lines. Grimly, the Rebels charged forward, slashed by bullets and artillery missiles. As one Rebel said, it was "an iron storm that threatened certain destruction for every living thing that would dare to cross." A second charge of Confederates followed the first, and Colonel Appler's nerve cracked. He yelled to his troops, "Retreat and save yourselves!" and ran for the river, followed by most of the Fifty-third Ohio.

By now, the Confederate charge had spread eastward and was pressing in on the Union line over a length of nearly four miles. Sherman, to the west of Shiloh Church, and Gen. Benjamin Prentiss to the east of it, clung desperately to their positions. Back in Corinth, at 8:00 A.M. Beauregard ordered the second wave of Confederates into action.

General Grant was still having breakfast at his Savannah headquarters when he first heard the cannons in the distance. "Gentlemen," he said to his staff, "the ball is in motion. Let's be off." First, he dispatched a brief note to Buell calling for reinforcements. Buell's army had begun arriving in Savannah, on the east bank of the river, the day before.

The Battle of Shiloh was one of the bloodiest in the Civil War. Confederate and Union lines continually broke and reformed throughout the first day, as countless soldiers on both sides lost their lives.

"We Are All Cut to Pieces"

At about 9:00 A.M., Grant reached the battle. The Union line was on the verge of collapse. Fresh units moving into the front lines ran into their comrades, who were "rushing back from the front

Lethal Ammunition

At the beginning of the Civil War, the largest artillery that either army had were "six-pounders"—cannons that fired six-pound cannonballs. Soon, though, foundries on both sides were turning out huge guns capable of launching ten-pound balls farther and more accurately than the old six-pounders. In addition to heavy iron cannonballs called solid shot, the new artillery also fired charged shells, case shot, and canisters. These were all loaded with powder and contained a fuse so they would explode after reaching their target. Shells burst into deadly fragments, while case shot and canisters contained iron balls that scattered with tremendous force when their containers exploded. Even more than the advances in rifle technology, the new artillery made the Civil War the deadliest of all American wars.

As the Civil War progressed, artillery became more sophisticated. At right are Union stockpiles of cannon (background) and mortar guns (foreground). (Below) The 13-inch, 8.5-ton mortar Dictator, largest of the siege guns at Petersburg, stood on a railroad flatcar and hurled missiles that weighed 200 pounds.

Confederate soldiers had thought the Battle of Shiloh was over when at dawn General Grant (center) led Union soldiers in an attack that would win the battle.

pell mell," as one soldier recalled, "holding up their gory hands, shouting 'You'll catch it! We are all cut to pieces! The Rebels are coming!'" Thousands of retreating Union soldiers raced to the river's edge, and many swam across to safety on the other side.

While the Union reformed its line about a mile behind its original position, the Confederate formation was in disarray. Some of the soldiers, who had not eaten in twenty-four hours, stopped to wolf down the breakfasts left on the fires in the Union camp and to collect souvenirs. The brief pause was a blessing for the Union troops, which used the time to regroup. Grant rode forward to visit Sherman, who was worried that they were outnumbered by the Rebels. "Well, not so bad," Grant replied, "Buell must be here soon."

The Horror of Battle

Meanwhile, the Confederate generals were confident, too. Beauregard had moved his headquarters up to Shiloh Church and was using Sherman's tent. Confederate soldiers remembered seeing the fiery little man standing on a stump by the church, wearing his lucky red cap and urging them on, sending troops off toward the heaviest fighting. He ordered heavy artillery brought forward, which was soon laying down a devastating fire on the new Yankee line. John T. Bell, a Second Iowa private, later recalled what it was like: "I am lying so close to Captain Bob Littler that I could touch him by putting out my hand when a shell burst directly in

Wounded in Battle

In a typical Civil War company of one hundred soldiers, there was one surgeon and two assistant surgeons. Removing the wounded from the battlefield was the job of company musicians and "soldiers least effective under arms." Others were expected to double as ambulance drivers. They drove horse-drawn wagons filled with injured men to military or general hospitals.

The casualties were so high, however, that this system was totally inadequate. Injured men were often left on the field of battle through the night, and many who could have been saved bled to death before they could be helped. One of Gen. George McClellan's lasting contributions to warfare was the establishment of the first official ambulance corps, which served the Army of the Potomac. Trained noncombat medical personnel wore special uniforms and risked their lives to reach the wounded in the midst of battle and evacuate them as quickly as possible to surgeons' stations at the rear of the battleground.

There were never enough surgeons, nurses, or medical supplies at the surgeons' stations to handle all the wounded. Surgery was still crude in the mid-1800s. The only anesthetic available was chloroform, which deadened the nerves slightly and made the patient drowsy. The most effective way to treat a badly wounded limb was to amputate it and apply a tourniquet to stop the bleeding. This usually stopped the infection caused by the lead bullets and shrapnel from spreading. There was no penicillin.

So many soldiers shot in the stomach or chest died from their wounds because there was no way to stop the infection from spreading. This explains, in part, why such a high percentage of wounded soldiers died. On the Confederate side, where medical supplies and personnel were even less adequate, 18 percent of the wounded died from their wounds. On the Union side, 14 percent died from their wounds. By comparison, in more recent wars, such as the Vietnam War, only one out of every four hundred wounded soldiers died.

A surgeon prepares to amputate the limb of a fallen soldier in this rare photograph of a Civil War field hospital. With very few ways of fighting infection, the most common method of "curing" a soldier who had suffered a wound to his limbs was to amputate.

Shiloh

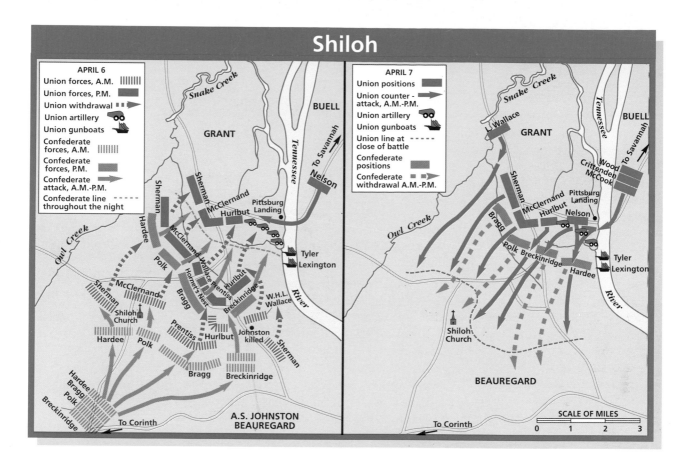

our front and a jagged piece of iron tears his arm so nearly off that it hangs by a slender bit of flesh and muscle."

On the Confederate right, Maj. Gen. Benjamin Cheatham thought the artillery fire would give him a chance to break through the enemy line. Cheatham's men came running at the Yankee line. When they reached a distance of 150 yards, the Union cannons opened fire. The lines of Confederate soldiers rippled and fell like grass cut down by a scythe. Still, the Rebels ran on, believing they could force the Yankee line to retreat. But the Yankee line erupted with gunfire. The Rebel charge was stopped 10 yards from the Union line.

There the bodies lay in piles. Some were headless, others limbless. Some had been cut in half by the cannon fire. Wounded men whimpered and groaned. One Confederate soldier stumbled out of the chaos and gasped, "It's a hornet's nest in there." The name stuck, and all the Rebels began calling the left flank of the Yankee line the Hornet's Nest.

The Confederate soldiers near the Hornet's Nest were now in a disorganized jumble. Many had become separated from their regiment and found themselves fighting under the wrong commander. With no clear orders coming from the rear, one commander after another attempted assaults on the Hornet's Nest.

Over the next two hours, the Confederates attempted four more piecemeal attacks on the Hornet's Nest, usually without the support of artillery. Each time, the assault was stopped. Perhaps as many as one thousand Confederate soldiers lay dead or wounded at that one spot, and they had not gained an inch.

When General Johnston finally appeared, he was enraged. Mounting his horse, he personally led a charge on a peach orchard just to the east of the Hornet's Nest. Moments later, Johnston was seen reeling in his saddle. An aide lowered the general to the ground and discovered that his boot was full of blood. A cannonball had nicked an artery in Johnston's right leg, and he bled to death before medical help could arrive. In his pocket was a tourniquet that could have saved his life, if anyone had thought to use it.

General Beauregard immediately assumed command of the Rebel army and ordered that Johnston's body be hidden from view and news of his death be kept secret so that the troops would not be demoralized. Then, he turned his attention to the troublesome Hornet's Nest. Elsewhere, the Yankee line was crumbling, but the Hornet's Nest had not fallen. After eleven or twelve full-scale charges against this one position, the Confederates still had not budged the Union forces there, which were under the command of General Prentiss.

Finally, Beauregard began calling in more cannons to fire on the Hornet's Nest. Within an hour, sixty-two cannons were lined up facing Prentiss's troops. At 4:00 P.M., they opened fire, and the Union flank began to fall back. General Prentiss raised the white flag of surrender and gave himself and his men up to the Confederates. By holding his ground through a dozen charges and scorching artillery bombardments for as long as he did, however, Prentiss gave General Grant time to form yet another line of defense along the Tennessee River.

After the Hornet's Nest collapsed, the Confederates spent a precious hour rounding up prisoners. As news of the capture spread, many Confederates believed that the majority of the Union army had been captured. Thousands of Rebel soldiers settled down at the Yankee camps, cooked Yankee food, and rummaged through the tents for blankets and supplies.

Elusive Victory

Wanting to make their victory complete, some of the Confederate commanders tried to rouse their troops to make one last drive to capture Pittsburg Landing in the remaining hour or so of daylight. "One more charge, my men," shouted Gen. Braxton Bragg, "and we shall capture them all!" But Bragg's men went into battle alone. General Beauregard had called a halt to the Rebel charge.

Angels of Mercy

"A military hospital is no place for a refined lady." This was the opinion of most Americans at the start of the Civil War. Even more degrading than work in a military hospital was being a field nurse. Traditionally, the women who volunteered their services to assist surgeons in the field were poor and uneducated and were not accepted into traditional society. Some of them worked not only as nurses but also as prostitutes.

The overwhelming need for medical aid in the Civil War began to change that situation. In the North, women like Clara Barton and Mary Ann Bickerdyke, fondly called Mother Bickerdyke, showed up on the field of battle and in the soldiers' camps to bring needed supplies and to comfort the wounded. When a surgeon once demanded of Bickerdyke what authority she had to be in a field hospital, she replied, "I have received my authority from the Lord God Almighty. Have you any higher authority?"

Clara Barton worked so close to the front lines that on one occasion at Antietam, a stray bullet passed through her sleeve and killed the soldier she was caring for. After the Civil War, Barton founded the American Red Cross Society.

Confederate women such as Kate Cumming organized thousands of "refined ladies" to volunteer to fill a dreadful shortage of nurses in Mobile, Richmond, and other Confederate cities. In the South, the image of a refined lady was even more rigid than it was in the North. Being in a military hospital was bad enough, but when Cumming decided to go directly to the army camps at Corinth, Mississippi, after the Battle of Shiloh, even her friends protested. "As to the plea of its being no place for a refined lady," said Cumming, "I wonder what Florence Nightingale and the hundreds of refined ladies of Great Britain who went to the Crimean War would say to that!"

In the hastily constructed hospitals in both the South and the North (above), women acted as nurses, cooks, morale-boosters, and letter writers. (Right) Clara Barton worked tirelessly on the battlefield to bring wounded men comfort and medical supplies.

These heavy guns made up the last line of defense at the Battle of Shiloh.

As Bragg's men clambered up a steep ravine, they were cut to pieces by Union artillery fire.

Finally, an aide to General Beauregard rode up to Bragg and cried, "The general directs that the pursuit be stopped; the victory is sufficiently complete." Bragg cried, in disbelief, "Was a victory ever sufficiently complete?" Learning that the other Confederate regiments had already withdrawn, Bragg lamented, "My God, My God, it is too late."

General Beauregard, spending the night in Sherman's tent, sent a wire to President Davis that evening: "A complete victory," it said. And it very nearly was.

Unlikely Cheers

By dusk, the Yankee soldiers were thoroughly exhausted and demoralized, and they waited for the worst. The worst, however, was over. Gradually, it became clear that the Confederates were not advancing any farther. Then, an odd thing occurred: the men began to cheer. They had been pushed to the very edge of the Tennessee River and had seen hundreds of their comrades killed or wounded, but the men began to cheer.

They cheered because they saw reinforcements, thousands of them, unloading from boats on the river shore. Buell's Army of the Ohio had finally arrived, and the Union line was again strong. The Rebels had lost their best opportunity to drive Grant out of Tennessee.

As darkness fell, a terrible night began. Most of the wounded Yankee soldiers had been left behind with the dead on the battlefield. During the Civil War, no organized system of medical teams existed to seek out and treat the wounded. So most hurt soldiers just lay there among the dead, writhing in pain, and burning with the fever and awful thirst that accompany gunshot wounds.

Young Wilbur Crummer of the Forty-fifth Illinois, lay exhausted in the Union camp that night, listening to the shrieks and groans of the wounded. "Some cried for water," he recalled, "others for someone to come and help them. I can hear those poor fellows still, crying for water."

Then a cold drizzle began, and by midnight it was a downpour, whipped by a hard, cold wind. Lightning lit up the ghostly field. The wounded crawled to each other for comfort and warmth and died huddled together. A number of wounded dragged themselves to a pond near the Hornet's Nest, where their blood turned the water red. Blood was everywhere on the field.

All night, the handful of surgeons in both camps worked. There were so many men to treat that they helped the most seriously wounded first, if they thought they could be saved. Bone saws rasped through the night, and by morning, piles of amputated limbs were stacked on the ground.

Most of the Confederates thought the battle was over. They assumed the Yankees would retreat across the river in the dark and be gone by morning. Beauregard received a report that Buell's army had marched away, and he did not send out any scouts to verify the report.

Confederate colonel Nathan Bedford Forrest was not so confident. He ordered some of his troops, dressed in captured Yankee uniforms, to sneak behind enemy lines and report back on the situation. They returned with reports of unit upon unit of fresh Yankee troops coming across the river to strengthen the Union troops.

Forrest rushed to tell his superiors. "If this army does not move and attack them between this and daylight, it will be whipped like hell before 10 o'clock tomorrow," he warned. His warnings were ignored.

That same night, Grant told Sherman that he planned to attack at dawn. "Beauregard will be mighty smart," he added, "if he attacks before I do." When dawn broke, Union troops moved forward. Grant had forty-five thousand men in the field, about half of them fresh. Beauregard could muster only twenty thousand men capable of fighting, none of them fresh.

When these Confederate soldiers awoke to the sound of gunfire, they must have felt deep dismay. They were exhausted, hungry, sore, and tired of fighting. As the day progressed, Grant's forces gradually wore them down, although not before encountering savage resistance around Shiloh Church. But the situation was hopeless for the Confederates. About 2:30 in the afternoon, Beauregard ordered a retreat. The Confederate army could easily have been routed or forced into surrender, but the Union soldiers were also weary, and Grant chose not to pursue.

William Tecumseh Sherman

In 1861, William Tecumseh Sherman was living in the South. With the start of the war, however, he resolved, "I will do no act, breathe no word, think no thought hostile to the government of the United States." As a graduate of West Point and a veteran of the Mexican War, he was recruited as one of the North's few experienced officers, along with his friend, Gen. Ulysses Grant. He served under Grant at Shiloh, Vicksburg, and Chattanooga and earned a reputation as one of the Union's bravest and most cunning generals. Though he was much like Grant in his informal manner and known to his troops as "Uncle Billy," his military strategy was different. While Grant usually drove directly at the enemy, undeterred by heavy casualties to his own army, Sherman favored outmaneuvering the enemy, as he did against Confederate generals Joseph Johnston and John Bell Hood in his conquest of Atlanta. He is perhaps remembered best for his brutal and destructive march to the sea, which left a broad swath of destruction from Atlanta to Savannah, Georgia. But when the war ended, Sherman offered Confederate armies opposing him more lenient terms of surrender than any other Union general.

Unlike most generals of his day, Sherman tried to minimize the number of casualties in battle. He did this by attempting to outmaneuver his enemy rather than charging headlong into Confederate lines.

Lingering Horror

The Battle of Shiloh had ended, but on the battlefield, scenes of the horror lingered for days. Grant reflected that bodies lay so close together that one could have walked over them for great distances without touching the ground. Each side lost about seventeen hundred men, and more than eight thousand men on each side were wounded in this one battle. The casualty reports were so shocking that even people in the North were outraged. Grant was severely criticized for allowing his army to be attacked in such a vulnerable position. Many people called for his resignation, but Lincoln said, "I can't spare this man, he fights."

The Confederate loss at Shiloh made it impossible to hold Corinth. Union troops commanded by Halleck arrived on the outskirts of Corinth on May 28, and they began to bombard the Confederate defenses. Beauregard knew that retreat was inevitable, but he first devised a deception that would allow his army to escape intact. Empty trains chugged in and out of town all day, accompanied by loud cheering, as if reinforcements were arriving. The ploy worked. Halleck hesitated until his troops heard the Confederates blowing up supplies that they could not take with them. On May 30, the Union took possession of an empty town.

Empty or not, the loss of Corinth was a serious blow to the Confederates. After a year of fighting, they had lost Missouri, Kentucky, and most of Tennessee. In addition, New Orleans, at the mouth of the Mississippi River, had been taken in a naval attack. This victory gave the Union an excellent port for delivering troops and supplies and for launching a campaign up the Mississippi toward the Confederate stronghold at Vicksburg. One Confederate soldier correctly assessed the significance of Shiloh when he said, "The South never smiled again after Shiloh."

CHAPTER FIVE

Robert E. Lee: A New Confederate Hero

The war had begun with great promise for the Confederacy in the spring of 1861 and somewhat ominously for the Union. This was especially true in Virginia, where the Rebels had twice turned back Yankee invasions. As time went by, however, Northern advantages began to tip the scale in its favor. In the West, the Confederates lost valuable ground in Tennessee. In Virginia, they had not actually lost a battle, but they seemed to be losing ground.

On March 7, 1862, Gen. Joseph Johnston, commander of the Confederate Army of Northern Virginia, ordered his troops to march out of Centreville, Virginia, and head about forty miles south to Fredericksburg, on the Rappahannock River. Johnston had two reasons for this self-imposed retreat—one strategic, the other economic.

Johnston reasoned that keeping his troops closer to Washington was no longer a strategic advantage. The capital had become so strongly fortified that there was little likelihood of mounting an attack on it. By staying within a day's march of Washington, McClellan's Army of the Potomac could attack with all its might, not having to leave many troops behind to defend the capital. By moving farther south, the Confederates could force the Yankees to divide their troops, leaving some to guard the capital and others to pursue the Confederates.

But Johnston's move may have been more the result of economic considerations. His army had spent a miserably cold, wet winter in northern Virginia. The Union naval blockade was beginning to have an effect in the South. Supplies of tents, clothes, shoes, and even food were dwindling, and prices were beginning to rise. Many of Johnston's troops had been living without adequate food and supplies for four months. Being positioned closer to Richmond would enable the Confederates to rotate and feed their soldiers more regularly.

Following the retreat of the Confederate army toward Richmond, General McClellan settled on a plan to attack Richmond. Once again, however, he greatly overestimated his enemy's numbers and decided against a direct march to Richmond. Instead, he orchestrated a massive movement of troops and supplies to the Union-held Fort Monroe at the tip of the Virginia peninsula, southeast of Richmond. Using the fort as a base of operations, McClellan then planned to march the sixty miles up the peninsula to Richmond.

McClellan had so many men and supplies that Confederate soldiers at Yorktown, the first obstacle in McClellan's path, were outnumbered by Union soldiers ten to one. The Confederate camp was manned by only eleven thousand men under Gen. John Magruder, but Magruder was cunning. By having his artillery fire at everything in sight and ordering a single company of several hundred men to march in a circle through heavy woods, in and out of the camp like an endless column of soldiers, Magruder convinced Yankee scouts that he had an enormous army.

McClellan feared that his "small" army of 100,000 would not have a chance. He wrote to Lincoln, "It seems clear that I shall have the whole force of the enemy on my hands, probably not

Just one of fifteen batteries McClellan put in position outside Yorktown. McClellan's obsessive fear of being outnumbered caused him to sit outside Yorktown and wait for the Confederates to leave, rather than attacking their inferior forces.

Messengers and Spies

Before the advent of radio, gathering and communicating information during a war were major problems. Most battles did not go as planned, simply because there was no effective way for commanders to communicate with their field generals. Most regiments included a signal corps, which used flag signals to send messages to other regiments before and during battles. Both the North and the South used lighted torches from towers atop their military headquarters in Washington and Richmond, respectively, to send messages.

The other problem commanders had with sending messages was spies. Spying was not very sophisticated during the Civil War, but it did not have to be. No one used secret codes or special devices for sending messages.

Interestingly, many women were formally used as spies by the militaries of both the North and the South. One well-known Confederate spy was Nancy Hart of Virginia. She was so well respected as a scout that the Union Army offered a large reward for her capture and she was arrested in July 1862. While in prison, Hart managed to get hold of her guard's musket, killed him, and escaped on a horse to join the nearest Confederate troops.

This photo shows the fortifications hastily erected by John Magruder to defend against McClellan's massive Army of the Potomac. Magruder had far too few soldiers to man his long line of defenses, but they succeeded in intimidating the timid McClellan.

less than 100,000 men, and possibly more." Therefore, he decided against a direct attack on Yorktown in favor of "the more tedious, but sure operations of a siege." In other words, McClellan with his 120,000 men set up camp outside Yorktown and aimed his artillery at the 11,000-man Confederate camp, contented to wait for them to retreat.

Eventually, McClellan's strategy worked. General Johnston ordered the Confederates at Yorktown to retreat to the Rappahannock. Gradually, the Union force continued its march on Richmond, defeating the Confederates in a major battle at Williamsburg. After his victory, McClellan continued to move so slowly that one of his own generals called him the "Virginia creeper." Still, by May 24, he was so close to Richmond that his soldiers could set their clocks by the chimes of the city's churches.

Robert E. Lee

A week later, the Army of Northern Virginia, under General Johnston, launched a savage attack on McClellan's forces, but they were unable to push the Union troops back. The battle was costly for both sides, but especially for the Rebels. Johnston was seriously wounded, leaving his army without a field commander. Jefferson Davis finally convinced Robert E. Lee to take the post, for the sake of his beloved Virginia.

Lee's army of fifty thousand men was situated west of McClellan's camp, which straddled the Chickahominy River outside of Richmond. The key to Lee's plan was to have the small Confederate army under Stonewall Jackson march south from the Shenandoah Valley on the morning of June 26 and outflank, or go around, the northern flank of the Union army. Then, as Jackson attacked from the north with his seventeen thousand men, Lee's army would sweep in from the west along the banks of the Chickahominy River.

Jackson Fails Lee

For reasons that have never been explained, Jackson never showed up on June 26. After waiting about six hours, Maj. Gen. A. P. Hill, Lee's youngest and probably least patient general, could stand to wait no longer. Without bothering to notify Lee, Hill took his division across the Chickahominy and, at about 5:00 P.M., launched the first attack against the Union's northern flank.

As might have been expected, the result was a disaster. Lee's first major engagement was a miserable failure. Of his men, 1,484 were killed or wounded. The Union had only 361 casualties, and McClellan sent an ecstatic telegram to Lincoln: "I almost begin to think we are invincible."

Despite McClellan's proclaimed confidence, he grew increasingly worried during the night about reports that a huge Rebel army led by Stonewall Jackson had arrived from the north. Finally, he ordered his northern flank to withdraw about four miles to the east to a less vulnerable position on Boatswain Creek.

The next morning, Lee showed another characteristic that made him different from his predecessors—and much like the Union's General Grant. Despite the setback, Lee did not retreat or alter his plan. Unflinching, he set out again to achieve his goal of cutting off McClellan's northern flank. When he discovered that the flank had moved to the east, he sent his four commands eastward in three roughly parallel columns. His intention was to hit the Union simultaneously from the front and the side.

Two hours later, Lee launched a general charge against the enemy line. When Gen. John Bell Hood—the bearded, fair-haired, thirty-one-year-old commander of the Texas Brigade—rode by, Lee singled him out. "Can you break this line?" he asked Hood. When Hood said he would try, Lee replied, "Then God be with you." The Texas Brigade marched across a swampy creek and up the slope beyond until the men were within ten yards of the Union line. Then, for the first time, they opened fire.

"That volley," remembered a Union officer, "was the most withering I ever saw delivered. The New Jersey Brigade broke all to pieces." Then, the whole Union line began to crumble. Soon, the Union troops were in full retreat.

Gen. A. P. Hill's impatience was to be his doom at Chickahominy.

McClellan astounded his corps commanders by announcing that the Army of the Potomac was retreating to the north bank of the James River. He was giving up his campaign to take Richmond, even though his forces still outnumbered the enemy by almost two to one. McClellan's retreat gave Lee what one of his officers called "the opportunity of his life," the chance to deal a severe blow to the Army of the Potomac, perhaps even force a surrender of some of its commanders. The opportunity slipped away, however, as once again, Stonewall Jackson was nowhere to be found when he was needed.

For two more days, Lee pursued McClellan's retreating army and tried to deliver the crushing blow. With fierce attacks on June 30 at Glendale and the following day at Malvern Hill, it appeared as though Lee might be able to surround the Union troops and force a surrender.

Not Knowing When to Give Up

But both times, the result was the same. Although Lee was a brilliant strategist and an inspiring leader, part of what made him great also made him vulnerable: he did not know when he had been beaten. On July 1, 1862, the Union forces occupied a position on top of Malvern Hill. Lee set up his artillery to the east and west and blasted the enemy with a blistering cross fire. Still, the Confederates were outnumbered and outgunned. All day, Lee sent division after division up Malvern Hill to overrun the Union line. Each time, they were crushed. Malvern Hill was the first time, but it would not be the last, that Lee senselessly wasted his army trying to achieve a hopeless objective.

Mercifully, darkness fell and the battle came to an end. Confederate losses were a staggering 20,614 casualties, compared to 15,849 for the larger Union army. But the new Confederate leader had accomplished his primary purpose: Richmond was safe, at least for the time.

McClellan's loss and withdrawal from Richmond shocked the North. It came as a blow to Lincoln, who just two months earlier had eagerly anticipated the defeat of the Confederacy. It also convinced the president that the time for a limited war was over. "The time has arrived when military authorities should be compelled to use all the physical force of this country to put down the rebellion," he declared.

Republican congressmen agreed. It was time for a full-scale assault not only on the battlefield but on the enemy's home front as well. In July 1862, Congress passed a confiscation act allowing Union soldiers to confiscate the property of any "traitor," which included any citizen of the Confederacy. This law empowered

Battle Hymns

In the 1800s, music played a big role in stirring the emotions of soldiers. Many Northern units marched off to battle singing, "John Brown's body lies a'moulderin' in the grave/But his soul is marching on." In 1862, Julia Ward Howe wrote the words to the "Battle Hymn of the Republic," to be sung to the same tune. It became the Union's unofficial battle anthem, especially after the Emancipation Proclamation.

The South, too, had its battle songs, the most famous of which was "Dixie." Soldiers sang, "In Dixie Land I'll take my stand/To live and die in Dixie!" One marching song that reflects the irony of the Civil War is the "Battle Cry of Freedom." Armies on both sides marched to this song.

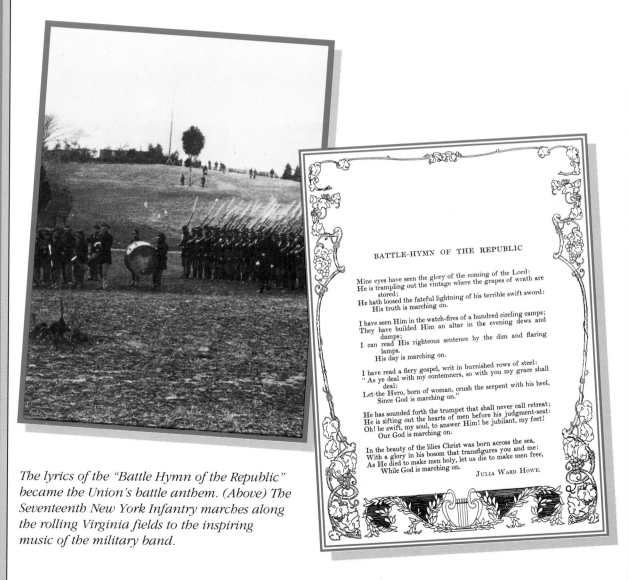

The lyrics of the "Battle Hymn of the Republic" became the Union's battle anthem. (Above) The Seventeenth New York Infantry marches along the rolling Virginia fields to the inspiring music of the military band.

Drummer Boys

Boys too young to join the army as soldiers sometimes joined as musicians. Mostly drum and fife players, these musicians accompanied regiments on marches. Many stories were told of drummer boys' bravery. One poem popular during the war centered on a drummer boy at the Battle of Vicksburg. On May 19, 1863, an assault was made on the town. Many Union soldiers died. During its progress, a boy came limping back from the front and stopped to speak to General Sherman. Although blood formed a puddle at his feet while he spoke, he said, "Let our soldiers have some more cartridges sir—caliber fifty-four." After delivering his message, he went back to his regiment.

Another young Union drummer boy who gained fame was Johnny Clem, who ran away to war before he was ten years old. Clem marched with the twenty-second Michigan Regiment to major battles at Shiloh, Murfreesboro, and Atlanta. It was at the Battle of Chickamauga in Tennessee, however, that the young drummer's exploits became legendary. There, a Confederate galloped toward him shouting, "Surrender, you little devil!" Armed with a musket that had been sawed off to fit him, Clem shot and wounded the officer, who was taken prisoner.

Union soldiers to remove slaves from their Southern owners. The law stated that slaves "shall be deemed captives of war and shall be forever free."

The Confederacy Weakens

In fact, the Confederacy's situation was getting worse. Even while it was winning battles on the battlefield, it was struggling to survive. With its smaller population and much more limited financial resources, the Confederacy would not be able to sustain its heavy losses much longer. Its superior generals could provide leadership, but they could not supply essentials like food and clothing.

General Lee realized that the Confederacy's greatest hope was to wear down the North's will to fight and force some kind of political compromise. The best way to discourage Northerners, he reasoned, was to take the war to them. As long as all the fighting and destruction took place on Southern soil, he believed, Northerners would not become alarmed. Even if he could not hope to hold Northern territory for long, Lee felt it was time to invade the North.

On to Maryland

Lee stood at the North's doorstep, just twenty-five miles from Washington. His next bold move would be to strike into the border state of Maryland. He wrote his intentions to President Davis: "The present seems to be the most propitious time since the commencement of the war for the Confederate Army to enter Maryland."

What he planned was only a brief drive into Maryland, by which he hoped to accomplish three things: He wanted to feed his starving army on Maryland's rich autumn harvest. He wanted to lure enough Union troops away from Virginia to prevent another enemy attack on Richmond. Finally, and perhaps most important, he wanted to strengthen the impression in the North that the Confederacy was not about to fold.

Informed of their general's intention to march into Northern territory, thousands of Confederate soldiers deserted. They had enlisted to defend their homeland, they protested, not to invade the North. Yet Lee believed that a Confederate show of strength in the North would further undermine the status of Lincoln and the Republican party. Already being attacked by the Democrats for not working out a compromise to avoid the war, Lincoln was being increasingly criticized for not being able to win it. If the Confederacy could somehow hold out until the next presidential election in 1864, Lincoln would almost surely lose. A new administration would be under strong pressure to end the war with the South.

It was a ragtag army of fifty thousand men that Lee led across the Potomac River into Frederick, Maryland, on the afternoon of September 4. Most of them were hungry, dirty, and unshaven.

Railroads at War

One important advantage the North had over the South throughout the war was its railroad system. When the war began, the North had about twice as many miles of railroad track as the South. This made it much easier for the North to move food, ammunition, and supplies from producers and manufacturers to the front lines.

Shortly after the beginning of the war, the North increased its advantage tremendously by commissioning Col. Herman Haupt to be field commander of the U.S. Military Railroads. Haupt was responsible for creating an efficient transportation network centered in Alexandria, Virginia, just outside Washington. From there, the Union could send supplies and troops by train to destinations along occupied railroad lines in Virginia, Tennessee, Alabama, and Mississippi.

The North's industrial advantage could clearly be seen in its railroads. With the creation of the United States Military Railroads, an agency developed to coordinate rail service, the North could transport supplies and men much more quickly. At left, Col. Herman Haupt inspects a crew working on the railroad.

Prisoners of War

During the war, about 194,000 Union soldiers were captured and sent to Confederate prisons in the South. The conditions in these prisons were so terrible that 30,000 of these soldiers died in prison, mostly from disease and starvation. The prisons were wet, cold, and unsanitary. Most were temporary clapboard barracks with dirt floors.

The most notorious Confederate prison was in Andersonville, Georgia. It had no barracks at all. In the fierce summer heat and through the cold, wet winter, prisoners here were kept in flimsy tents. Food rations consisted of a single meal of watery soup each day. In less than one year, more than thirteen thousand prisoners died at Andersonville.

The Union's prison camps were better equipped than the Andersonville prison, but rations were still meager. Conditions on both sides were ideal for spreading diseases such as flu and pneumonia. Of the 214,000 prisoners taken by the Union, 26,000 died in prison.

Soldiers bury their own in a long trench that would soon be filled with the dead at Andersonville. For the dead, at least, the suffering was over.

A rare photograph shows the miserable conditions at Andersonville. Filthy, starving prisoners of war suffer the crowded conditions at the camp.

Abraham Lincoln visits the troops at Antietam.

They wore tattered, flea-infested uniforms. By one estimate, one-fourth of them had no boots and marched barefoot. Lee reminded the men who marched to Maryland with him that "none but heroes are left."

He chose to make his first stand in the North at Sharpsburg, a little Maryland town twelve miles north of Harpers Ferry, Virginia. James Longstreet was the first Confederate general to have his troops in place, just east of Sharpsburg in front of a meandering little stream called Antietam Creek. They were to be joined there on Tuesday, September 16, by Lee's heroic but starving troops.

McClellan's force of seventy thousand men arrived at Antietam Creek on Monday, before most of Lee's forces left Harpers Ferry. If he had attacked Longstreet right away, McClellan could have overwhelmed the Rebel troops. But McClellan spent that Monday analyzing the field and attending to every detail of proper troop deployment. By the time he was ready to attack at dawn on Wednesday, Lee had his full force of forty thousand men strung along Antietam Creek for four miles.

Antietam

The Battle of Antietam Creek began when Union troops led by Gen. Joseph Hooker attacked the north end of the Confederate line, near Dunker Church, a small brick church so named because its members practiced baptism by dunking parishioners in the creek. Just north of the church, Stonewall Jackson and Jeb Stuart awaited the Yankee attack.

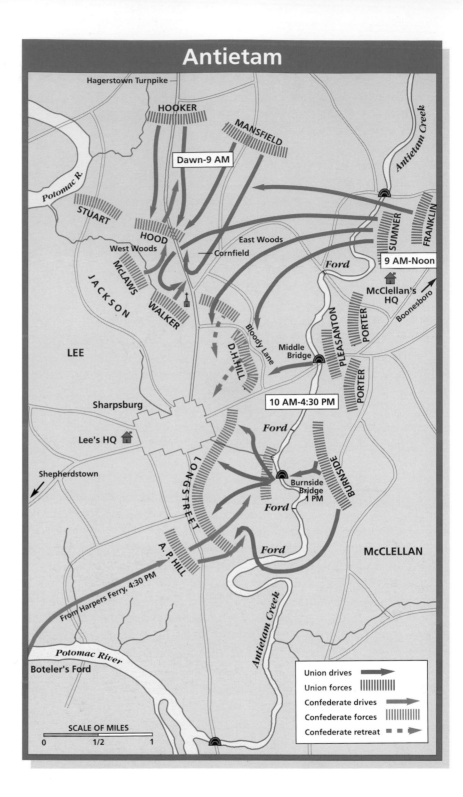

Antietam

HOOKER

MANSFIELD

Dawn-9 AM

Hagerstown Turnpike

Potomac R.

STUART

HOOD

West Woods

East Woods

Cornfield

McLAWS

WALKER

JACKSON

LEE

Sharpsburg

Lee's HQ

Shepherdstown

A. P. HILL

From Harpers Ferry, 4:30 PM

Potomac River

Boteler's Ford

Antietam Creek

SUMNER

FRANKLIN

9 AM-Noon

McClellan's HQ

Boonesboro

Ford

PLEASANTON

PORTER

PORTER

D.H.HILL

Bloody Lane

Middle Bridge

10 AM-4:30 PM

Ford

Ford

LONGSTREET

BURNSIDE

Burnside Bridge 1 PM

Ford

McCLELLAN

Antietam Creek

SCALE OF MILES

0   1/2   1

Union drives
Union forces
Confederate drives
Confederate forces
Confederate retreat

The Confederates had taken cover in the cornfields of the David Miller farm. The stalks of corn stood taller than their heads, so the soldiers did not bother to crouch or lie down. But Hooker's scouts detected the brilliant reflection of sunlight on the bayonets standing erect among the cornstalks. The Union cannons opened fire, leveling the stalks of corn and hundreds of Rebel soldiers at the same time. This twenty-acre cornfield soon became known simply as the Cornfield. As the day wore on, it became the scene of the fiercest fighting in Antietam, which would be remembered as the single bloodiest day in the Civil War.

The two lines surged back and forth through the Cornfield's broken and bloodstained stalks no fewer than fifteen times during the course of the day. By 9:00 A.M., after four hours of intense fighting, more than eight thousand Americans, about half Union and half Confederate, had been killed or wounded. As the battle raged on, General Lee seized the initiative, forcing McClellan to react. About twenty-five hundred Rebels held a superb defensive location on a country lane at the base of a hill. The lane was so worn by erosion and wagon traffic that it lay several feet below the level of the surrounding fields. Known to locals as Sunken Road, it made a perfect trench for Rebel soldiers to lie in wait for the Yankees to approach.

From that day forward, Sunken Road became known as Bloody Lane. The Rebels lay in wait there while the Union

Federal troops charge through the Cornfield at Antietam. Union and Confederate troops would surge back and forth through the field all day, leaving the stalks blood-stained and broken.

A Zoave regiment of Union soldiers charges the Confederates outside Dunker Church. (Right) The grim sight of Bloody Lane following the Battle of Antietam. These men defended their position to the last, giving Union troops the time they needed to rally a defense.

troops came over the hill a hundred yards away and started toward them. Col. John B. Gordon of the Sixth Alabama recalled vividly what happened next:

> Now the front rank was within a few yards of where I stood. With all my lung power I shouted, "Fire!" My rifles flamed and roared in the Federals' faces like a blinding blaze of lightning accompanied by the quick and deadly thunderbolt. The effect was appalling. The entire front line, with few exceptions, went down in the consuming blast.

Dead artillerymen lie near Dunker Church after the Battle of Antietam.

Before his rear lines could recover from the terrific shock, my exultant men were on their feet, devouring them with successive volleys.

Line after line of Union troops fell back on the long slope in front of Bloody Lane that morning. Finally, however, because they had so many more men, the Union troops forced the Confederates to retreat from Bloody Lane. The Rebels' heroic stand at Bloody Lane gave General Longstreet time to set up twenty cannons and assemble a line of defense just west of Hagerstown Turnpike. Longstreet's cannons held off the Union advance for a time, but he was desperately low on ammunition. A major thrust by the Union troops would have split Lee's army and probably doomed it. McClellan had the extra men available, too, waiting in reserve a mile east of Sunken Road. Shaken by his losses and fearing that Lee might counterattack at any moment, however, McClellan refused to commit his reserves, and the opportunity was lost.

Mathew Brady

The Civil War was the first war to be photographed, and it brought all the horror of the battlefield to the front pages of newspapers and magazines.

The most famous and most prolific of these photographers was Mathew Brady. In October 1862, following the Battle of Antietam, Brady put together a series of photographs of unknown Confederate corpses on a battlefield at Antietam. They were the first photos ever taken of dead Americans on a field of battle, and they made the public abandon the idea that war was romantic. "Let him who wishes to know what war is look at this series of illustrations…Mr. Brady has brought home the terrible earnestness of war. If he has not brought bodies and laid them in our dooryards, he has done something very like it," wrote Dr. Oliver Wendell Holmes Sr.

Ironically, Brady's photographs, which continue to inspire and awe, could have been lost forever. Brady originally had over 7,000 pictures. The expense of taking these, which he did at his own cost, ruined him. One set of photos finally was purchased by the government, but the amount paid to Brady by Congress did not pull him out of poverty and he died in a New York hospital in the 1890s, poor and forgotten.

Burnside

Instead, McClellan now sent orders to Gen. Ambrose Burnside to bring his eleven thousand men to attack the Rebels' southern flank at Sharpsburg.

Lee watched nervously as the Union force, outnumbering his own by four to one, moved closer. The fate of his army, perhaps of the Confederacy, rested on the outcome of this encounter. Their only hope was a powerful column of reinforcements reported to be en route from Harpers Ferry.

An hour later, with the Battle of Antietam hanging in the balance, Lee was still peering into the southeast looking for some sign of the reinforcements. All he could see were the long blue lines of Burnside's advancing army. Suddenly, in the distance, a gray-clad column appeared, flying the Virginia and Confederate flags.

The reinforcements immediately plunged into a cornfield and hit the Sixteenth Connecticut Regiment. The gun smoke in the cornfield was so thick that it was hard to tell friend from enemy. To make things even more difficult, many of the Confederates arriving from Harpers Ferry had stolen new Union uniforms from the Union supply depot there.

After the Connecticut troops broke and ran, General Burnside ordered a withdrawal of his entire corps, even though he still had about eighty-five hundred men left, or twice the number of enemy troops now confronting him. The Battle of Antietam was over. Men on both sides had prayed for darkness to put a stop to the slaughter. Never before had so many Americans fallen in combat in a single day. In all, casualties numbered about twenty-three thousand, with more than fifty-five hundred killed.

The Emancipation Proclamation

More than half of the killed and wounded at Antietam were Union soldiers, but the battle was a modest victory for the Union. Lee's army, badly depleted, was forced to withdraw from Maryland back to Virginia. Lee's invasion of Maryland had lasted two weeks. In Washington, Lincoln welcomed the news of the Rebel retreat, and he sought to take full advantage of it. On September 24, 1862, he publicly announced that he planned to issue the Emancipation Proclamation. Unless the Confederate states returned to the Union by January 1, 1863, he declared, "all slaves held in the rebel states shall be then, thenceforward, and forever free."

Ironically, the proclamation freed all slaves in the Confederacy but not those in the border states that had remained loyal to the Union. By exercising his war powers to seize enemy resources in the South, Lincoln was able to free the slaves there. He had no similar constitutional power to act against slavery in states loyal to the Union. The Emancipation Proclamation symbolized how much the president's view of the war had changed since April 1861. Instead of a limited war to restore the Union, it had become an all-out war in which "the old South is to be destroyed and replaced by new propositions and ideas."

On New Year's Day in 1863, Lincoln issued the Emancipation Proclamation. On the signing of this historic document, Lincoln spoke these words:

> Fellow citizens, we cannot escape history.... The fiery trial through which we pass, will light us down, in honor or dishonor, to the latest generation.... The dogmas of the quiet past, are inadequate to the stormy present.... In giving freedom to the slave, we assure freedom to the free. We must disenthrall ourselves, and then we shall save our country.

Two weeks after Antietam, Lincoln visits McClellan in an effort to urge the general to use his troops to end the war quickly.

The proclamation freed 3.5 million black slaves in the South and made as many as half a million black men eligible to serve in the Union army. Both of these actions enhanced the Union's advantage in the war and dealt a crushing blow to the South. Also, the Emancipation Proclamation was met with such approval in Great Britain and France that the Confederacy could no longer hope for help from those countries.

After its strategic victory at Antietam, however, the Union let another golden opportunity slip by. A vigorous pursuit of the Confederate army immediately after its retreat from Maryland could have destroyed it. But General McClellan did not pursue. Inexplicably, he remained camped in Maryland while Lee hurried back to Virginia to regroup.

McClellan's Ambitions

Lincoln was so frustrated by McClellan's strategy that on October 4, 1862, he visited McClellan personally in the field at the Union camp near Sharpsburg, Maryland. Upon Lincoln's urging, McClellan finally began to move his army south. It soon became clear, though, that it was a slow, halfhearted effort on McClellan's part.

Rumors spread through Washington that McClellan was purposefully stalling. It was well known that the general had political ambitions and that he favored a negotiated settlement of the war that would allow the Confederate states to return to the Union as slave states. McClellan would have the best chance to implement his plan if the war were still being fought in 1864. Then, the Northern states, sickened by a long and costly war, would welcome the Democratic party's proposal for negotiations. And they would welcome McClellan as the Democratic candidate for president.

The rumor of McClellan's betrayal was soon spreading through Washington. Whether true or not, it was the last straw

General Lee surveys the battlefield at Fredericksburg on December 13, 1862.

for Lincoln. On November 5, 1862, Lincoln removed McClellan as commander of the Army of the Potomac and replaced him with General Burnside.

Burnside was a loyal soldier, but on the field of battle, he proved no match for Robert E. Lee. Under Burnside's leadership, the Army of the Potomac continued to lose key battles to the smaller and poorly equipped Army of Northern Virginia.

During the winter of 1862, Lee's army camped in the town of Fredericksburg, Virginia, on the Rappahannock River, and Burnside stationed his troops just across the river. For more than four weeks, Confederate and Union soldiers fought little.

Then, on the morning of December 11, the Union opened fire with about one hundred cannons aimed at the city. The Battle of Fredericksburg began. It engaged more Americans than any other single battle in this country's history.

The main Confederate defense was set on a ridge overlooking Fredericksburg from the west known as Marye's Heights. There, Union and Confederate forces were pitted in a vicious struggle. The key to the Confederate position was a lane at the foot of Marye's Heights. The lane was bordered by a four-foot-high stone wall that made a perfect fortress. From behind the wall, Confederate infantrymen could stand and fire at the onrushing Yankees. Behind them, Confederate artillery were massed. So well covered was the approach to Marye's Heights that one Confederate colonel said, "A chicken could not live on that field when we open on it."

They opened on it, too, as soon as Burnside sent his men charging up Marye's Heights. Wave after wave of blue uniforms attempted to reach the walled lane. The closer they came to the wall, the thinner the wave of blue became before it fell back. In all, Burnside sent seven divisions to attack the Confederate position but could not get the Rebels to budge. About seven thousand Union soldiers were killed or wounded, and not a single soldier reached the stone wall. As a bitter cold night approached, the Union retreated back to Fredericksburg and the surrounding plains. From there, they could hear the Rebels cheering and rejoicing in their victory.

Union soldiers could also hear the moans from the thousands of wounded still lying on the ground in the bitter cold. They cried for help, for water, for their mothers, and for death to relieve their agony. One Union officer described it as "a smothered moan that seemed to come from distances beyond reach of the natural senses."

Union wounded lie in the field at Marye's Heights. In Francis Miller's Photographic History, *he eloquently describes the scene: "This is war. The man in the foreground will never use his right arm again. Never again will the man on the litter jump or run. It is sudden, the transition from marching bravely at morning on two sound legs, grasping your rifle in two sturdy arms, to lying at nightfall under a tree with a member forever gone."*

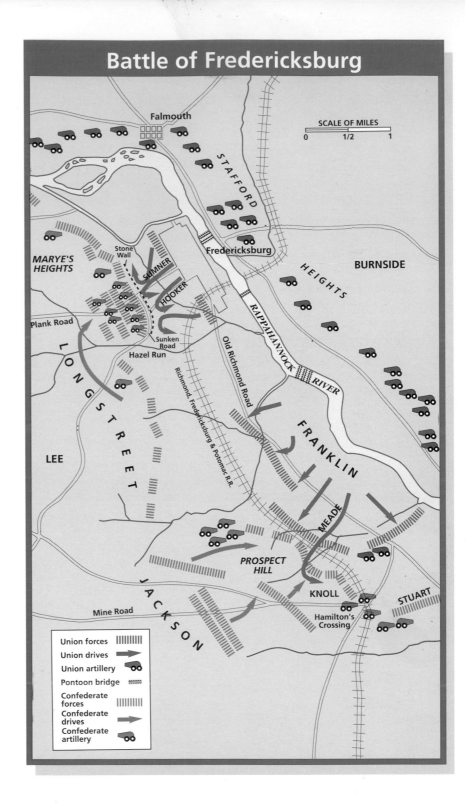

Battle of Fredericksburg

Falmouth

SCALE OF MILES

0   1/2   1

STAFFORD

Fredericksburg

HEIGHTS

BURNSIDE

MARYE'S
HEIGHTS

Stone
Wall

SUMNER

HOOKER

RAPPAHANNOCK

Plank Road

LONGSTREET

Sunken
Road

Hazel Run

RIVER

Old Richmond Road

Richmond, Fredericksburg & Potomac R.R.

LEE

FRANKLIN

MEADE

PROSPECT
HILL

JACKSON

Mine Road

KNOLL

Hamilton's
Crossing

STUART

Union forces ||||||||||

Union drives ➡

Union artillery 🔫

Pontoon bridge ░░░░

Confederate forces ||||||||||

Confederate drives ➡

Confederate artillery 🔫

The next morning, the Union troops retreated from Fredericksburg back across the Rappahannock. General Burnside decided to waste no more time or soldiers trying to chase General Lee. On January 20, 1863, he issued a proclamation: "The auspicious moment seems to have arrived," he declared, "to strike a great and mortal blow to the rebellion, and to gain that decisive victory which is due to the country." As a band played "Yankee Doodle," the Army of the Potomac marched off once again to conquer Richmond. Almost immediately, the fog moved in. By dark, rain had begun to fall. The rain continued for nearly four days. By the time it stopped, the army was so exhausted from tromping through mud that there was nothing to do but call off the campaign, which became known to cynical Northerners as the Great Mud March.

Burnside's officers condemned their commander for his poor judgment. Lincoln again decided to replace the commander of the Army of the Potomac. He offered the position to Gen. Joseph Hooker, who had been one of Burnside's loudest critics.

A Demoralized Army

The army that Hooker took over in February 1863 was weary, discouraged, and tired of defeat. It had not had a victory since Antietam, nearly five months earlier. And General Burnside had proven as inept at managing the army as in leading it to battle. The army's supplies were a disaster. There was a shortage of proper food, and living conditions were unsanitary. Thousands of men suffered from scurvy, dysentery, and other diseases. Many of the soldiers had not been paid in six months, and they were deserting by the thousands.

To his credit, General Hooker improved conditions for his army. He enforced sanitation regulations and improved food rations. He made certain that fresh bread, onions, and potatoes were available several times a week. These measures quickly cut the rate of illness in half.

Hooker also took steps to discourage desertion. He made sure that Congress paid the soldiers their back pay. He granted regular leaves of absence and filled the empty hours of camp life with drills and instruction periods.

At Chancellorsville, Virginia, Hooker bore down on Lee. His army of 100,000 men was twice the size of Lee's. Lee, however, when faced with this distinct disadvantage, divided his forces. It was a daring gamble, against all military logic, but it turned out to be Lee's masterstroke, and he often used this tactic. Hooker was completely fooled. For the next two days, even though his troops had an overwhelming numerical advantage, Hooker did not overtake the Confederate troops. His confusion led to another catastrophic and embarrassing loss for the Army of the Potomac.

Still, Hooker was in a position to defeat Lee's army. His generals encouraged him to attack Lee again the next day, but Hooker ignored them and ordered the entire army to withdraw.

Although the Battle of Chancellorsville (above) was a victory for the Confederate army, it was also a loss. Thirteen thousand Confederate soldiers were either killed, wounded, or missing. The Confederacy could not withstand the loss of so many men.

The victory at Chancellorsville was one of the Confederate army's proudest moments.

Yet every Confederate victory came at an extremely high price, perhaps unaffordably high. At Chancellorsville, thirteen thousand more Confederate soldiers were killed, wounded, or missing. While Lee could not afford any of these losses, one was more dear than all the rest.

The Death of Jackson

On the evening of May 2, after a successful attack, Stonewall Jackson rode forward with several of his staff officers to scout the enemy lines. As they returned to their own lines, pickets mistook them for Union cavalry and opened fire. Jackson was hit in the left arm, severing an artery just below the shoulder. He was taken immediately to a field hospital at Wilderness Tavern, and his left arm was amputated just below the shoulder. Then he was moved to a hospital ten miles south of Fredericksburg.

At first, Jackson seemed to be recovering from the amputation, but then pneumonia set in, a disease for which there was no cure. Informed of Jackson's condition, General Lee sent this message: "Tell him to make haste and get well, and come back to me as soon as he can. He has lost his left arm, but I have lost my right."

On Sunday, May 10, while his hospital room was filled with bright spring sunshine, Stonewall Jackson said in a firm, quiet voice, "Let us cross over the river and rest under the shade of the trees." And then he died.

Jackson's body was taken to Richmond, and he lay in state at the Confederate Capitol. Then, the body was transported to the Virginia Military Institute in Lexington, where Jackson had taught before the war. There, he was buried under the shade of the trees.

CHAPTER SIX

Closing the Vise

Fortunately for the North, the strategy first laid out by Gen. Winfield Scott in 1861 emphasized that victory in the West was at least as important as victory in the East. Union armies in the West, led by generals Ulysses Grant, William Tecumseh Sherman, William Rosecrans, and others, were slowly gaining control of the South's major rivers and railroads. This disrupted the flow of supplies in the western two-thirds of the Confederacy and isolated it from Virginia and the eastern coast. At the same time, Union superiority at sea was making it difficult for the South to carry on any kind of foreign trade. The Union navy's capture of New Orleans in the spring of 1862, coupled with Grant's victories in Tennessee the same spring, gave the Union control of the northern and southern extremes of the Mississippi River.

The heart of the river, however, still belonged to the Rebels. They controlled traffic on the Mississippi between Baton Rouge, Louisiana, and Memphis, Tennessee. Three Rebel strongholds were the key to their control: Memphis; Port Hudson, Louisiana; and Vicksburg, Mississippi. In the fall of 1862, the Union took the first two with surprising ease, but Vicksburg seemed insurmountable.

The city possessed natural defenses in all directions. It stood on a high bluff over the eastern banks of the Mississippi River. Walls armed with artillery along these bluffs rose as high as three hundred feet above the river. West of the river lay the swamps and bayous of Louisiana. To the east of Vicksburg, the bluff quickly descended to the plains of Mississippi. The steep bluff discouraged an attack from that direction. The city seemed so impenetrable that the military governor of Vicksburg announced proudly that "Mississippians do not know how to surrender."

Late in October 1862, General Grant decided to teach them. He led his army on a long march along the Mississippi from Memphis to Vicksburg. At the same time, Grant sent General Sherman's thirty-thousand-man army down the Mississippi by boat. For the next four months, Grant and Sherman tried every strategy and trick they could think of to gain control of Vicksburg. During those four months, though, Grant sat at his headquarters near Milliken's Bend, fifty miles north of Vicksburg, puffing cigars and thinking.

The result was a plan so preposterous that even Sherman, his most trusted friend, fiercely opposed it. Grant proposed that he personally lead an army of thirty-three thousand men down the west bank of the Mississippi about twenty miles south of Vicksburg to New Carthage, Louisiana. From there, he proposed crossing to the other side and attacking Vicksburg from the south.

The problems with Grant's plan were obvious. The Confederate army had sixty thousand troops at Vicksburg, positioned in an almost impenetrable fortification high on a bluff. Grant had only thirty-three thousand men, and only about one-third of

William Tecumseh Sherman, center, with his generals.

Ulysses S. Grant

In 1861, Ulysses S. Grant was living in Cairo, Illinois, without a job. He had served with distinction in the U.S. Army during the Mexican War, but after the war, he was forced to resign because of his reputation as a drunkard. As a civilian, he had gone from one business failure to another.

When the Civil War broke out, Grant was eager to get back into the army, but his requests for a commission were not answered. Grant persisted, and finally, in the summer of 1861, he was commissioned to take over the Twenty-first of Illinois, a newly formed regiment that was in a state of chaos. The fact that Grant was given a generalship at all is one indication of how desperate the Union army was for experienced officers. "Within a very few days," wrote one of the soldiers in the regiment, the new commander "had reduced matters in camp to perfect order."

Grant soon showed that he possessed a characteristic that was unusual among Union generals. He was quick to act, sometimes even impulsive. He did not analyze every move meticulously before he made it. Once he had a goal, he just chose the most direct way to achieve it. Over the course of the war, Grant demonstrated some brilliant strategy. Most often, however, his strategy was simple: "In warfare the one who strikes first usually wins."

General Grant's tenacious will to win the war for the Union was the great difference between him and the generals who had preceded him.

them could be transported across the river at one time. Once ashore, there was no way of supplying his army and no practical route of retreat open to him. All of Grant's plans depended on keeping the Confederate forces confused.

After marching his men to New Carthage, Grant selected a spot twenty miles farther downstream for a crossing. Before making the crossing, however, he sent a division of soldiers to a location one hundred miles north of Vicksburg, another to Youngs Point, northwest of Vicksburg, and a two-thousand-man cavalry unit on a raiding expedition through Mississippi and Louisiana. The cavalry did not capture anything, except the attention of the Confederate general in command at Vicksburg, John Pemberton.

With all of these diversions going on at once, Grant succeeded in getting his troops across to the Vicksburg side of the river. "I felt a degree of relief," he wrote in his diary, "scarcely ever equalled since." He was hardly out of danger, though. He was outnumbered in enemy territory and cut off from his supplies.

Instead of marching directly north to Vicksburg, where he would have been detected, Grant headed northeast toward the city of Jackson, Mississippi. He took Jackson and cut off the railroad that supplied Vicksburg, twelve miles to the west.

This photograph shows part of the honeycombed entrenchments built by federal troops during the siege of Vicksburg. Union soldiers were able to slowly creep forward by digging these trenches in advance of their front line positions. In this way, the Union was able to overcome Vicksburg's natural defenses.

General Grant and Union troops lay siege to Vicksburg, which lies in the distance.

On May 14, Sherman moved toward Vicksburg from the north. When Pemberton's Rebel forces ventured out of Vicksburg to cut off Sherman, Grant seized the opportunity. He pursued Pemberton's men relentlessly until they fell into a full-scale withdrawal back to Vicksburg. Grant's troops were now joined by Sherman's, and before the Confederates could mount a counterattack, the Union had established a camp on the bluffs north of Vicksburg.

Together, Grant and Sherman had galloped far ahead of their troops until at last they stood on the bluffs. There, Sherman turned to Grant. Until that minute, he said, he had doubted Grant's strategy. "This, however, is the end of one of the greatest campaigns in history, even if Vicksburg should somehow elude capture."

It was a triumphant moment for Union troops—their first major victory since Antietam nearly seven months earlier. It was an equally gloomy and bewildering one for the Confederates and for the stunned citizens of Vicksburg. It was a Sunday that no one in that town would soon forget.

Even though Pemberton had sent half of his men out of Vicksburg to stall other Union attacks, he still had a powerful force of thirty thousand men. He was not ready to surrender to Grant and Sherman's combined force of forty-five thousand.

Thousands of Pemberton's men marched into the streets among their beaten and demoralized comrades. According to local resident Mary Loughborough, "The men swung their hats, and promised to die for the ladies, never to run, never to retreat."

The Mississippians still had not learned how to surrender, but Grant had the city surrounded. After a few futile efforts to break through the fortified city, he resolved to take Vicksburg by siege—to simply surround the city and not allow supplies in or out. General Halleck had sent Grant reinforcements and so Grant was able to place a ring of seventy thousand soldiers around the city. No food, supplies, or troop reinforcements could reach Vicksburg. A Confederate soldier observed grimly, "A cat could not have crept out of Vicksburg without being discovered."

The siege of Vicksburg lasted for forty-eight days. During that time, more than two hundred Union cannons continually shelled the city from land while gunboats directed frequent bombardments from the river. Grant also ordered tunnels dug under the Confederate entrenchments and filled with explosives. Even these did not do enough damage to weaken the defense of Vicksburg.

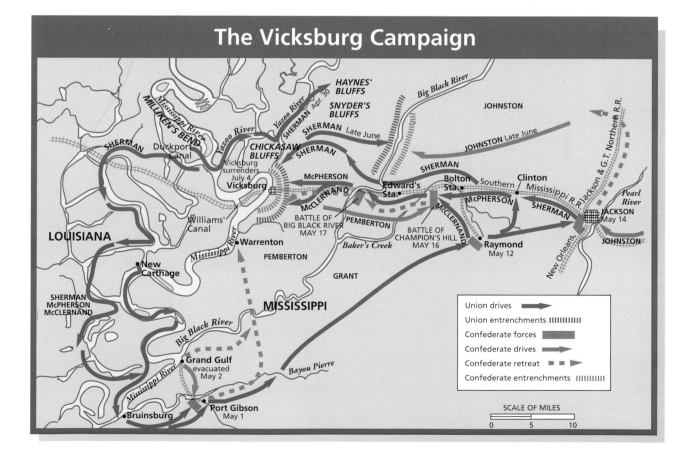

The Vicksburg Campaign

Legend	
Union drives	➤
Union entrenchments	||||||||||
Confederate forces	▬
Confederate drives	➤
Confederate retreat	▪ ▪ ▪ ➤
Confederate entrenchments	||||||||||

SCALE OF MILES
0   5   10

Entrenchments

Civil war leaders were at first reluctant to use entrenchments and fortifications in battles. The manual labor required to build them was thought to be below the dignity of the soldier. Opinions at the time held that entrenchments were cowardly and that soldiers should stand out in the open and fight. As the deadly speed and accuracy of new Civil War weapons took their toll in mounting casualties, however, Civil War officers realized that the methods for fighting with these weapons had to change. Standing in open fields, just a few yards from the enemy, no longer worked.

Both armies, therefore, began to build earthworks around their defensive positions. These began as primitive dirt mounds, but they gradually evolved into more elaborate earth and log fortifications. Some were even complete with bombshelters.

The Confederates, with their inferior numbers, found entrenchments particularly useful. They would dig themselves into rifle pits, hide their artillery in gun pits, and make their positions virtually impregnable. In order to give the illusion of strength, Confederates would also add "quakers" to their entrenched lines. These were logs shaped like cannon. From a distance, the enemy was unable to tell the quakers from real cannon.

Pictured here are three Confederate soldiers who have been taken prisoner after the Battle of Gettysburg. Undersupplied, the Confederates had no uniforms to wear and were lucky to secure decent shoes.

It was the shortage of food and water in Vicksburg that finally forced the Confederates to surrender on Independence Day, July 4, 1863. It was a great day for the Union forces. While Confederate forces were surrendering in Vicksburg, troops under Robert E. Lee were retreating from Gettysburg, Pennsylvania. These two events, taking place almost one thousand miles apart, sealed the fate of the Confederacy.

The War in the East

Although the actions in the West were vital in determining the outcome of the war, it was the war in the East that attracted most newspaper and magazine reporters, photographers, and therefore, the attention of most Northerners and Southerners. As late as June 1863, the popular opinion was that the Union did not have a general who could match Lee. Despite enormous advantages in troops, supplies, and weapons, the North had squandered countless opportunities to defeat Lee's Army of Northern Virginia and capture the Confederate capital at Richmond.

With each lost opportunity, the Democratic party in the North gained new followers. The shift from a limited war to preserve the Union to a full-scale war to free the slaves had also left many Northerners disenchanted. Former commander of the Army of the Potomac, George McClellan, led the opposition to Lincoln's

"war of emancipation." The longer the war lasted, the more people turned against Lincoln because they saw more Union soldiers being killed or wounded. A growing number of Northerners believed that it would be impossible to completely subdue Lee and the Confederates.

Lee, too, was confident that his army could whip any Union army, even if his men were outnumbered. He was so confident that he often refused to consider the odds against him. So in June 1863, he decided to invade the North a second time. Once again, his goal was not to occupy Northern land for long but to further discourage Northerners. Lee figured that if he could just hold out for another year against the North, inflicting heavy losses while keeping his own at a minimum, the majority of Northerners would vote Lincoln out of office in 1864. In his place, they would probably elect McClellan or another Democrat who would seek a compromise settlement to end the war.

On June 21, 1863, Gen. Jubal Early led the first Confederate company into Pennsylvania. Early marched as far north as Wrightsville on the Susquehanna River. On the way, he marched through Gettysburg, Pennsylvania, and sent word back to Lee that the town had a shoe factory, where the Rebels could probably steal some badly needed footwear.

On June 28, George G. Meade succeeded Joseph Hooker as commander of the Army of the Potomac. The following day, he

The battle at the little town of Gettysburg, Pennsylvania, was unexpected. Round Top can be seen at the extreme right of this photo. (Bottom) George G. Meade replaced Joseph Hooker as the commander of the Army of the Potomac.

set off for the Susquehanna in pursuit of Lee's army. Before he reached his destination, his path crossed Lee's at Gettysburg, about ten miles north of the Pennsylvania border.

If it were not for this chance encounter, the quiet south-central Pennsylvania town that was home to a Lutheran seminary and Pennsylvania College (now Gettysburg College) would be as little known today as it was then.

The area surrounding Gettysburg has the perfect layout for a Civil War battle. West and south of the town are two parallel ridges about three-quarters of a mile apart. Immediately south of Gettysburg lies Cemetery Hill, named for the nearby Evergreen Cemetery. From Cemetery Hill, Cemetery Ridge extends south for nearly two miles before it terminates in two knoblike hills: Little Round Top and beyond it, Big Round Top. Three-quarters of a mile west of the Round Tops, another ridge rises and runs north, parallel to Cemetery Ridge, for about five miles. This is Seminary Ridge, on which the three-story, red-brick building of the Lutheran seminary stands, directly west of town. Beyond this, Seminary Ridge ends northwest of Gettysburg at Oak Hill and Oak Ridge. These long lines of hills and ridges were ideal places for Civil War generals to position their troops.

On June 30, 1863, when a Union cavalry division under Gen. John Buford entered Gettysburg at about 11:00 A.M., the townspeople were frantic. Just minutes before, a Confederate infantry brigade had come through town. Not realizing that Meade's Army of the Potomac was so nearby, the leader of the Rebel brigade, Gen. Henry Heth, was planning to return to Gettysburg the next day to raid the shoe factory.

Early the next morning, July 1, Heth rode back toward Gettysburg. While still about 1.5 miles west of town, he came to a small, winding creek named Willoughby Run. Beyond the creek was McPherson's Ridge, which was just south of Seminary Ridge. Heth saw something he did not like on top of McPherson's Ridge—a division of Union soldiers. But he still did not guess that this was part of the Army of the Potomac.

The First Shots

Heth ordered his soldiers forward toward the Yankees, who opened fire with small cavalry artillery. The first shots of the Battle of Gettysburg had been fired. Hearing the gunfire, reinforcements for both sides marched toward McPherson's Ridge. Soon, a full-scale battle, which neither side had planned, erupted west of Gettysburg.

Throughout the day, Lee, who was camped northwest of Gettysburg with the largest share of his army, was at an unusual disadvantage. His cavalry, under Jeb Stuart, usually kept him informed of the enemy's positions and vulnerable areas. But

Confederate and Union soldiers face each other down at the Battle of Gettysburg.

Stuart, not expecting a major battle at Gettysburg, was off on his own raid of southeastern Pennsylvania. Without Jeb Stuart's cavalry, Lee was poorly informed about the enemy he was facing. He did not even realize until late on July 1 that the Union troops were part of the Army of the Potomac.

One of the Confederates spotted Union soldiers wearing the distinctive black felt hats of the Black Hat Brigade, or Iron Brigade. He shouted, "There are those damned black-hatted fellows again! 'Tain't no militia. It's the Army of the Potomac!" General Lee, who was still nowhere near Gettysburg, would not be happy with that news. He had not wanted a confrontation with the 100,000-man army, at least not so soon.

The Union army had been equally surprised, however, and Confederate troops, who occupied the high ground to the north and west, were pushing them back toward Gettysburg. The Union line was wilting under the waves of Confederate charges. The Union's feared Iron Brigade had defended McPherson's Ridge boldly all day. But of its nineteen hundred men, only eight hundred remained standing. The rest had been killed or wounded.

Meanwhile, north of Gettysburg, Gen. Jubal Early led his Confederate troops down from Wrightsville, and they entered the battle with resounding artillery fire, sending shock waves along the entire Union line. One by one, lines of Union troops went streaming back through Gettysburg. One of Early's officers commented, "It looked as if the end of the war had come."

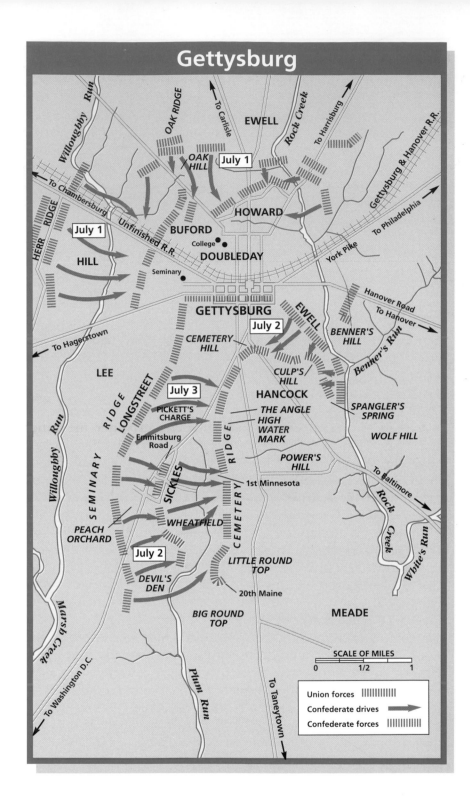

Gettysburg

As the Rebels gained the upper hand, however, the absence of Jeb Stuart's cavalry became particularly costly. Lee, not knowing the enemy strength or positions, could not devise a clear strategy. Every move had to be decided as the battle unfolded.

Three Confederate divisions commanded Seminary Ridge. Two of the three generals favored pressing forward and pushing the Yankees back through Gettysburg and into the hills beyond. The third, however, Gen. Richard Ewell, refused to advance without direct orders from General Lee, and the Rebels lost a great opportunity. Late that afternoon, an aide finally arrived with orders from Lee to push forward and take the high ground beyond Gettysburg. By that time, however, Ewell decided it was too late in the day to begin a major attack.

Lee's Timing Is Off

With a chance to regroup, the Union troops set up their defenses on top of the ridges south of Gettysburg. Gen. Winfield Scott Hancock, thirty-nine years old, was the man temporarily in charge of the Union troops at Gettysburg. Hancock set artillery at Cemetery Hill, just south of the city, and prepared to defend it against the next Confederate charge. But that charge did not come. Lee's timing, for once, was off, and one can only speculate how sorely he missed Jeb Stuart's cavalry that day.

By dawn on the second day of the Battle of Gettysburg, the Yankees were dug in, waiting for the Rebels to attack. Lee planned a series of attacks, one immediately after the other, starting with his southernmost wing and moving gradually northward. At the far south of Lee's line was Gen. John Bell Hood's Texas Brigade. Hood headed out through Devil's Den, a jumble of huge boulders, and on toward Big Round Top. Lee believed that this strategic spot was the key to a Confederate victory. If a few pieces of artillery could be brought up the hill, they could blast the enemy line from one end to the other.

Meanwhile, Union commander Meade had been so concerned with defending the north end of his line that he had left Big Round Top virtually unprotected. Hood's brigade reached the 305-foot summit with relative ease, experiencing just one serious loss: during the march up Big Round Top, General Hood had been wounded. His replacement, Gen. Evander Law, wanted the brigade to move from Big Round Top and seize the even more strategic Little Round Top, about half a mile to the north.

Little Round Top was also undefended, but Union brigadier general Gouveneur Warren just happened to climb Little Round Top in time to see the Texas Brigade advancing toward it. Moments before the Confederates reached the hill, Warren managed to direct a Union brigade up Little Round Top. The soldiers of the Twentieth Maine Regiment positioned themselves among the rocks and waited for the Texans to approach. Over the next three hours, Union and Confederate soldiers clashed in the battle for control of Little Round Top. In the end, the Twentieth Maine lost 130 of its 386 men, but they had valiantly held the far left

Gen. John Bell Hood led his Texas Brigade through Devil's Den at the Battle of Gettysburg.

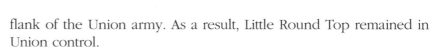

The Union makes its final charge at Cemetery Hill (Above). The Confederates were in an impossible position. As they tried to take the hill, Union soldiers mowed them down. (Right) The dead lie scattered on the rocky slope of Little Round Top.

flank of the Union army. As a result, Little Round Top remained in Union control.

Nowhere in the four years of the Civil War was the fighting more fierce than at Gettysburg. The soldiers of the Union Army of the Potomac had been pummeled by the Army of Northern Virginia time and again. This time, they were determined to defeat the Rebels. This time, for a change, the Rebels were the invaders, and the Union soldiers were fighting to defend their home.

One area where the fighting was most intense was in the Peach Orchard and Wheat Field just west of Little Round Top. Into these fields General Longstreet threw his Confederate division against the Union line commanded by Gen. David Birney. All day, the two sides battled in the Peach Orchard and the Wheat Field. Control of Wheat Field changed hands six times. The scene in that field haunted Pvt. Robert Chase of the Twenty-second Massachusetts Regiment for the next fifty years of his life:

The hoarse and indistinguishable orders of commanding officers; the screaming and bursting of shells, canisters, and shrapnel as they tore through the struggling masses of humanity; the death screams of wounded animals; the groans of their human companions; wounded and dying trampled underfoot by hurrying batteries; riderless horses and the moving lines of battle. A perfect hell on earth, never perhaps to be equalled, certainly not to be surpassed nor ever to be forgotten in a man's lifetime. It has never been effaced in my memory, day and night for fifty years.

Late in the afternoon, Longstreet's men won control of the Wheat Field and the Peach Orchard. The Union's real strength, however, was up on Cemetery Ridge. Longstreet exhausted the remainder of the day in a series of disjointed and unsuccessful assaults on Cemetery Ridge. One of Lee's staff members later admitted, "There was an utter absence of accord in the movements of the several commands."

Gen. Richard Ewell, who was supposed to be leading a Confederate assault on Culp's Hill and Cemetery Hill from the north, failed to attack for the second time in as many days. This freed Union troops facing Ewell to aid their comrades along Cemetery Ridge. There, the battle raged late into the night.

Lee had tried attacking the ridge in a sequence of charges all day. On the third day of the Battle of Gettysburg, he was determined to throw all of his strength at the ridge in one massive assault from the west. Longstreet would approach from the right, Ewell from the left, and the troops of Gen. George Pickett from the center. The next morning, just as Pickett's three brigades began to take their position on Seminary Ridge, Lee heard gunfire from Culp's Hill on his left. The Union had already disrupted his timetable.

Lee had not expected the Union to attack, but it had started the day with a bombardment of Ewell's forces. Ewell's men, finally engaged, fought hard, but they were outmanned and were forced to withdraw.

That left only Longstreet and Pickett to attack the Yankee position on Cemetery Ridge. At the foot of the ridge was a lane bordered by a stone wall. General Meade, anticipating Lee's attack, amassed thirty thousand soldiers along and behind the wall. Cemetery Ridge seemed like an impenetrable fortress, but General Lee did not waver from his plan.

An Impossible Position

There was hardly an officer or a foot soldier present at Gettysburg who did not see how difficult the Confederate position was. A clearing 1.5 miles wide stood between them and the Yankees.

After marching across that clearing, the outnumbered Rebels would have to overtake the Yankees, who had lines of cannons along the top of Cemetery Ridge and thousands of riflemen at the foot of it, waiting behind the stone wall.

Lee ordered Longstreet to prepare for a direct assault. Longstreet, who had been Lee's most loyal general and faithful friend, protested bitterly. He estimated that they had about fifteen thousand men to use in the assault. Longstreet made a final, impassioned plea against the attack:

> General, I have been a soldier all my life. I have been with soldiers engaged in fights by couples, by squads, companies, regiments, divisions, and armies, and should know, as well as anyone, what soldiers can do. It is my opinion that no 15,000 men ever arrayed for battle can take that position.

Lee refused to budge. As Longstreet recalled, "I said nothing more. Never was I so depressed as upon that day." The man who was to lead the Confederate charge was Gen. George E. Pickett. Never before had General Pickett led troops into battle, yet this one charge would bring him lasting fame. Reluctantly, Longstreet gave Pickett the order to form a front that extended northward from the Peach Orchard along the face of Seminary Ridge. Behind the Confederate men, he lined up 170 cannons.

As some of Pickett's men waited nervously in the field, a startled hare ran out in front of them. One of the men said, "Run you ol' hare. I wish I were a hare and I could run from here, too." The men knew that what lay ahead for many of them was the horrible death on the battlefield that most of them had witnessed a thousand times.

Why did General Lee, the man usually considered the most brilliant general on either side, order such a suicidal assault? Longstreet later recalled that Lee's "blood was up. And when his blood was up, there was no stopping him or changin' his mind." Also, Lee had come so close to victory on the two previous days that perhaps he could not bear the thought that he had lost the opportunity to win at Gettysburg. Historian Stephen B. Oates explains the folly of Pickett's charge as a result of Lee's illusion that he and his army were unbeatable: "He had pummeled one Union general after another and had defeated or at least fought to a draw with the Army of the Potomac in almost every battle up to that point. Lee really did believe that if he asked his boys to do something, they would do it—that they would do anything. He had come by Gettysburg, then, to believe in his invincibility and that of his men. It was his doom."

At precisely 1:00 P.M., General Pickett gave the command. "Up men and to your posts. Don't forget today that you are from old Virginia," he told them. Then, the roar of artillery

A soldier lies dead in the Devil's Den after the Battle of Gettysburg.

burst the silence. Despite the noise, however, the Confederate bombardment was largely ineffective. With their targets obscured by clouds of smoke, most of the Confederate cannons shot high over their targets. As one Union soldier recalled, "All we had to do was flatten out a little thinner, and our empty stomachs did not prevent that."

At about 3:00 P.M., Pickett decided that the time for his charge had arrived. Unaware that most of the artillery fire had flown over the Yankees, Pickett rode to Longstreet and asked if he should advance. Longstreet, too discouraged to speak, merely bowed his head, and Pickett replied, "I shall lead my division forward, sir."

A Sea of Gray Turns Red

Like a sea of gray, twelve thousand Confederate soldiers marched in rank across more than a mile of open ground toward Cemetery Ridge. Yankee soldiers held their fire until the Rebels were within fifty yards of the stone wall. Then, the artillery opened up from the ridge, and the swarm of gray grew thinner. Entire companies of the gray-clad soldiers disappeared at a time. Only one company of about two hundred men made it past the stone wall. Every one of them was killed, wounded, or captured almost immediately. A Yankee soldier remembered what it was like coming face-to-face with his enemy in those frenzied moments.

The Gettysburg Address

On November 19, 1863, the Gettysburg battlefield was dedicated as a national cemetery, honoring the soldiers from both sides who had fallen there. Edward Everett, an elderly statesman from Massachusetts, was asked to give the main speech at the dedication service. President Lincoln was invited, almost as an afterthought, to "say a few words."

Everett spoke first that day, for one hour and fifty-seven minutes. Then President Lincoln rose and stepped to the podium. He spoke for two minutes, and when he finished, the large crowd gathered there was silent. Returning to his seat, he said to Everett, "It didn't scour well," meaning that the speech had not gone over well. Everett heartily disagreed. As he told Lincoln later, "I should be glad if I came as near to the central idea in two hours as you did in two minutes."

The crowd's silence was not from disapproval. Rather, they were stunned, struck by the eloquence of this simple speech that compressed into less than two hundred words the essential reason for this conflict: the preservation of democracy. The Gettysburg Address, which in Lincoln's opinion was a failure, became the most famous of his speeches. It has been memorized by millions of American schoolchildren for more than a century.

Lincoln addresses the crowd at Gettysburg Cemetery on November 19, 1863.

Fourscore and seven years ago our fathers brought forth on this continent a new nation, conceived in liberty and dedicated to the proposition that all men are created equal.

Now we are engaged in a great civil war, testing whether that nation or any nation so conceived and so dedicated can long endure. We are met on a great battle field of that war. We have come to dedicate a portion of that field, as a final resting-place for those who here gave their lives that that nation might live. It is altogether fitting and proper that we should do this.

But, in a larger sense, we can not dedicate—we can not consecrate—we can not hallow—this ground. The brave men, living and dead, who struggled here, have consecrated it, far above our poor power to add or detract. The world will little note, nor long remember, what we say here, but it can never forget what they did here. It is for us the living, rather, to be dedicated here to the unfinished work which they who fought here have thus far so nobly advanced. It is rather for us to be here dedicated to the great task remaining before us—that from these honored dead we take increased devotion to that cause for which they gave the last full measure of devotion—that we here highly resolve that these dead shall not have died in vain—that this nation, under God, shall have a new birth of freedom—and that government of the people, by the people, for the people, shall not perish from the earth.

Men fire into each other's faces not five feet apart. Bayonet thrusts, sabre strokes, pistol shots, men going down on their hands and knees, spinning round like tops, throwing up their arms, gulping blood, falling, legless, armless, headless. There are ghastly heaps of dead men.

After the ill-advised charge, Pickett met Lee, who told him to prepare his division for a possible counterattack by the enemy. "General Lee," Pickett answered, "I have no division now."

There was to be no counterattack. General Meade, deciding that his Union army was too exhausted to pursue the enemy, issued a proclamation commending his army for its "efforts to drive from our soil every vestige of the presence of the invader."

On July 4, neither side moved. They seemed stunned by their enormous losses. The Army of the Potomac had suffered twenty-three thousand wounded or dead. Lee's army had lost about twenty-eight thousand—nearly six thousand in Pickett's final charge. At about 1:00 P.M., lightning cracked, and the skies opened in a drenching downpour. As one man put it, "It washed the blood from the grass."

When Lincoln later read General Meade's account of the battle, ending with his proclamation to "drive the invader from our soil," he slapped his knee in anger. "My God, is that all?" he groaned. Lincoln had been trying for more than two years to convince his commanders that their goal should be the destruction of the Confederate army. He did not understand why Meade had not pressed the attack after Pickett's disastrous charge.

It may be true that the Union had let another opportunity slip away to crush Lee's army. On the other hand, Gettysburg was the Army of the Potomac's finest moment, and it changed the course of the war. In fact, Lee's army was so badly depleted by the Battle of Gettysburg that it would never recover.

July 4, 1863, was indeed a bitter day for the Confederacy. On the same day that Lee's defeated troops were marching back to Virginia, General Grant's victorious troops were marching into Vicksburg, Mississippi. The Mississippi River was one of the Confederacy's most important lifelines. After it was cut off, Grant and Sherman moved systematically from west to east, occupying Confederate territory and destroying railroad lines. With their victory at Chattanooga in October 1863, they gained control of the Tennessee River, the last major river in the West open to Confederate supply barges.

The following spring, as Grant and Sherman sat on the banks of the Tennessee planning their march to Atlanta, Grant received a telegram from the president. He was to report to Washington immediately—as the commander of all the Union armies.

CHAPTER SEVEN

The Death of the Confederacy

On March 8, 1864, a scruffy, bearded Union officer in a dirty, rumpled uniform appeared with a thirteen-year-old boy at the front desk of the Willard Hotel in Washington, D.C. and asked for a room. The clerk, thoroughly unimpressed, said the only thing available was a small second-floor room. The man said that was fine and signed the register, "U.S. Grant and Son, Galeena, Illinois."

As soon as the clerk looked down and saw the name, he realized his mistake. He immediately assigned General Grant the best suite in the hotel, the one where President Lincoln had stayed before his inauguration. Ulysses S. Grant had become a celebrity. That evening, Grant attended a reception at the White House, and the two men from Illinois, the president and the general of the Union armies, met for the first time. "Why here is General Grant!" exclaimed the president when he saw Grant arrive. "Well, this is a great pleasure, I assure you."

The next day, pleasure gave way to business. After Gettysburg, Lincoln had been disappointed in Gen. George Meade's cautious pursuit of Lee. It reminded him, said Lincoln, "of an old woman trying to shoo her geese across a creek." Grant decided that Meade would stay on as commander of the Army of the Potomac but Grant himself would map its strategy, not from Washington but from a tent next to Meadc's.

Grant named General Sherman to take his place as commander of the western armies. Then, he took a train to Cincinnati to meet with Sherman and discuss strategy. Later, General Sherman summarized the grand plan they had devised: "He was to go for Lee and I was to go for Joe Johnston. That was the plan."

Grant's orders to General Meade were equally brisk: "Wherever Lee goes, there you will go also." As springtime approached and the generals planned their campaigns, the soldiers in the ranks also knew what lay ahead. Grant's reputation for seeking victory at any cost was no secret. They knew that this was to be the summer of victory or death. No other option was acceptable to Grant.

One Union private wrote in a letter to his parents:

> The summer days are almost here, when we shall be wearily plodding over the roads once more in search of victory or death. Many a poor fellow will find the latter. I dread the approaching campaign. I can see horrors insurmountable through the summer months.

Grant's pursuit of Lee started in May 1864. He began with more than 120,000 men in the Army of the Potomac, compared to Lee's 60,000. For the entire summer and fall, Grant kept Lee on the move. His strategy was simple. With a vast superiority in arms and troop strength, he just kept hitting at Lee until he could finally deliver the knockout punch.

The two armies traversed the same regions of northern Virginia that they had been fighting over for the last three years: Fredericksburg on the Rappahannock, Chancellorsville, and the wilderness between these two cities. The South had only two assets with which to counter Grant's relentless pursuit: General Lee and a familiarity with the land.

General Grant and General Meade sit on church pews hauled outside of Massaponax Church for an impromptu meeting after Spotsylvania. Grant sits cross-legged beneath the trees, smoking a cigar. Meade sits at the far end of the pew at left, studying a map.

Philip Henry Sheridan dealt a mortal blow to Confederate forces when, in a clash with Confederate cavalry, Sheridan's forces mortally wounded Jeb Stuart.

For a while, that appeared to be enough. In three days at the Battle of the Wilderness, Lee's army handed the Army of the Potomac a staggering seventeen thousand casualties. These great losses did not seem to affect Grant. His predecessors would have surely retreated, but Grant seemed unperplexed. He instructed a correspondent who was about to depart for Washington to tell the president "that whatever happens, there will be no turning back."

The next morning, as the Union troops trudged drearily out of the wilderness, a call made its way up the Union lines: "Give way to the right!" Charging ahead of the troops was a small cavalry headed by General Grant himself on his horse, Cincinnati. The men tossed their hats in the air and gave a loud cheer. Grant had assured them that their suffering in the wilderness was not going to be wasted. Instead of retreating as they had in the past, they were moving deeper into enemy territory. "Our spirits rose," one veteran recalled. "That night we were happy."

The Rebels, too, were in high spirits. But as Lee moved his forces to cut Grant off again, he received some dispiriting news. Lee's cavalry commander, the dashing Jeb Stuart, had been killed in a clash with Union cavalry led by Gen. Philip Sheridan. Lee, usually a calm and composed man, confessed, "I can scarcely think of him without weeping."

Lee had little time to mourn, however. By June 3, Grant had moved his forces farther east, near the Chickahominy River, where the Battles of the Seven Days had occurred almost exactly two years earlier. Grant continued to batter away at Lee's army. Grant lost another seven thousand men at Cold Harbor and did not gain a foot of enemy ground.

Still, Grant ordered another attack. But this time, he was met by blunt refusals from his officers and men alike. Capt. Thomas

The grisly remains of the dead at Cold Harbor are gathered by black infantrymen. Blacks were often dealt the distasteful duty of gathering the war dead.

Cruel Arithmetic

Rifles and artillery too advanced for the outdated battle strategies and a shortage of trained military officers helped make the Civil War the bloodiest war in American history. In incidents like Pickett's charge at the Battle of Gettysburg, companies of one hundred to two hundred men charged forward as a unit, and as many as 80 or 90 percent of them were wounded or killed. At Gettysburg, the Twenty-sixth North Carolina Regiment of 1,000 men suffered the worst casualties for a complete regiment in a single battle. In this one battle, 588 of the 1,000 members of the regiment were wounded, and 86 men were killed. At the Battle of Petersburg on June 18, 1864, the First Maine Artillery Regiment had 210 out of approximately 1,200 men killed.

With more than 50,000 casualties in three days, Gettysburg was by far the bloodiest battle of the war. Lee's Army of Northern Virginia had 28,063 casualties at Gettysburg, out of an entire army of less than 70,000. More than 3,000 of them fell in Pickett's last, futile charge. The bloodiest single day of the war occurred on September 17, 1862, at Antietam, where casualties for both sides totaled 22,726.

A Civil War cemetery in Alexandria, Virginia is silent testimony to the thousands of soldiers who died in America's bloodiest war. At right, just one of the thousands of men who died fighting his own countrymen.

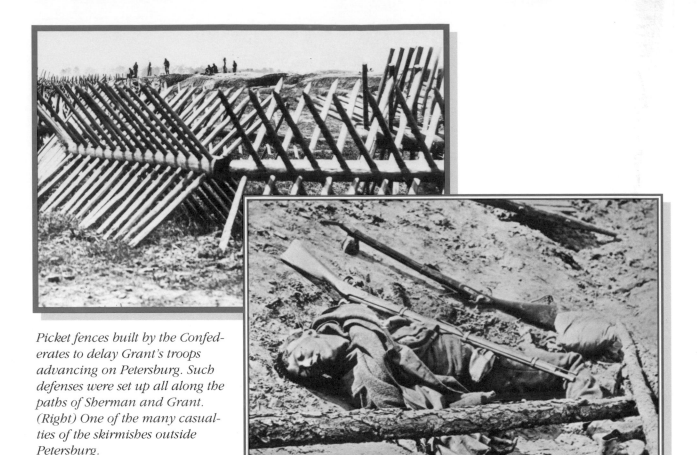

Picket fences built by the Confederates to delay Grant's troops advancing on Petersburg. Such defenses were set up all along the paths of Sherman and Grant. (Right) One of the many casualties of the skirmishes outside Petersburg.

Barker shouted, "I will not take my regiment in another such charge if Jesus Christ himself should order it!" Faced with such solid opposition from his own troops, Grant finally agreed to alter his strategy. He even offered an apology of sorts to his staff: "I regret this assault more than any one I ever ordered."

In less than a month, Grant had lost an unheard-of fifty thousand men. Despite the appalling numbers, he remained convinced that he could wear Lee down, with time. Lee had lost thirty thousand troops, and he could not bring in new recruits as rapidly as Grant could. For one thing, Grant had a brand new source of recruits: free blacks.

Although Grant seemed to lose battle after battle, at least in the casualty count, he had actually pushed Lee into a position only about twenty-five miles north of Richmond. Now, Lee could not move without exposing Richmond. With the South in this vulnerable position, Grant demonstrated that he could match Lee not only in his tolerance for casualties but in strategy as well.

He caught Lee by surprise by moving farther east, across the Chickahominy River. Once safe on the other side, he began marching his army south, not to Richmond but beyond, to the city of Petersburg, Virginia, twenty-three miles south of Richmond. From there, he could harm Lee by cutting off the railroad traffic that delivered arms, ammunition, food, and uniforms from Atlanta to Richmond. After a few more futile attempts to drive Lee's army out of Petersburg, Grant settled on the same siege strategy that had worked so well at Vicksburg. The siege of Petersburg began, and it would last until the closing days of the Civil War.

While Grant was closing in on Lee in northern Virginia, General Sherman was marching through the heart of the Confederacy from the west. Sherman's principal objective was to capture Atlanta, the industrial hub of the Confederacy. Here, arsenals and factories turned out most of the Confederacy's war supplies—rifles, cannons, ammunition, and uniforms.

The army that stood in Sherman's way was Gen. Joseph Johnston's Army of Tennessee. Sherman had the same kind of numerical advantage over Johnston as Grant had over Lee. Sherman's strategy, however, was far different. Unlike his superior, Sherman had little taste for bloody, all-out assaults that simply wear down an outnumbered enemy. "Its glory is all moonshine," he declared. "Even success the most brilliant is over dead and mangled bodies, with the anguish and lamentation of distant families." Instead, Sherman carried out a series of sly maneuvers, jabbing at the right and then driving past his enemy on the left with lightning speed.

Over the next two months, Sherman steadily pushed Johnston back across nearly one hundred miles of rugged Georgia hills. General Grant lost fifty thousand men by driving head-on against Lee in Virginia, but Sherman lost only twelve thousand by slipping past Johnston at every turn. By mid-July, Sherman was in position to attack Atlanta. A disappointed Jefferson Davis removed Johnston from command of the Army of Tennessee and replaced him with John Bell Hood.

Hood's responsibility was to defend Atlanta, but observing that Johnston had lost so much ground by not going on the offensive, Hood did not wait for Sherman to attack Atlanta. Instead, he sent troops from Atlanta out to engage the stronger enemy. In ten days, beginning on July 22, 1864, Hood lost one-third of his army of sixty thousand—more than twice as many as Johnston had lost in the previous two months.

Whenever he attacked Sherman's troops, the delighted Sherman would gloat, "They'll only beat their own brains out." One night, near the battle site, a Yankee picket called out to a Confederate across the way: "Well, Johnny, how many of you are left?" "Oh," came the reply, "about enough for another killing."

In the meantime, Sherman began the siege of Atlanta. In August, he began pouring artillery shells into the city, killing at least six private citizens. Hood sent Sherman a message protesting the bombardment of a civilian population. Sherman replied tersely that the citizens of Atlanta were traitors to the Union, and since the city housed an important military arsenal, the bombardment would continue.

Sherman received another message, though, that did alter his plans. It was from President Lincoln. The 1864 presidential election was approaching, and Lincoln feared that he was about to be voted out of office. His successor appeared to be none other than ex-general George McClellan, who was campaigning on a promise of peace with the South. Lincoln advised Sherman that only a decisive Union victory could preserve his administration and, in Lincoln's opinion, the Union itself. He expected Sherman to deliver that victory.

In the final week of August, General Hood observed that Sherman's troops were disappearing from their trenches around Atlanta. He was convinced that Sherman was in full retreat. On August 30, Hood learned the truth. Sherman was not retreating; he had marched deeper into Georgia. His troops were rapidly closing in on Jonesboro, some twenty miles south of Atlanta, where Sherman set his sights on a key depot of the Macon and Western Railroad.

By the time Hood could send troops to Jonesboro, the Union soldiers were firmly entrenched there. The Confederates attacked, but the only result was a costly defeat. Atlanta was now trapped, with its lifelines cut off in every direction. The next day, Hood ordered his troops to evacuate Atlanta.

The results of Sherman's bombardment can be seen in this photo taken of the ruins of Atlanta.

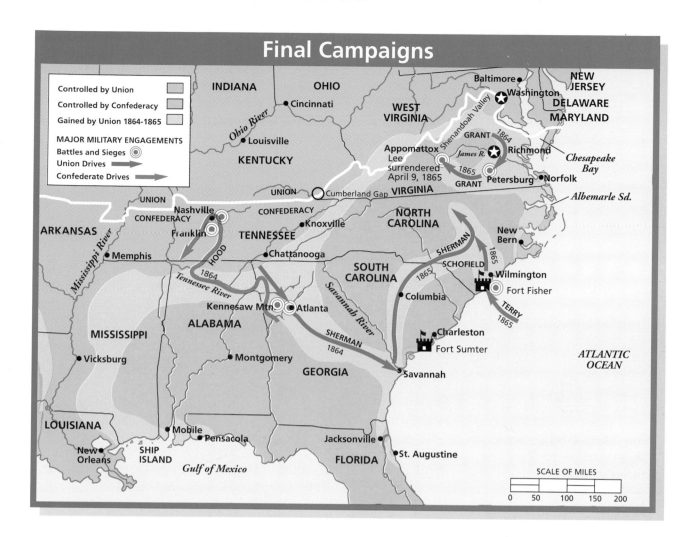

Final Campaigns

Controlled by Union
Controlled by Confederacy
Gained by Union 1864-1865

MAJOR MILITARY ENGAGEMENTS
Battles and Sieges
Union Drives
Confederate Drives

INDIANA
OHIO
Cincinnati
Baltimore
Washington
NEW JERSEY
DELAWARE
MARYLAND

WEST VIRGINIA
Ohio River
Louisville
KENTUCKY

GRANT 1864
Appomattox
Lee surrendered April 9, 1865
Richmond
James R.
Chesapeake Bay
Shenandoah Valley
1865
GRANT
Petersburg
Norfolk

UNION
Cumberland Gap
VIRGINIA
Albemarle Sd.

UNION
CONFEDERACY
Nashville
CONFEDERACY
Franklin
Knoxville
NORTH CAROLINA
New Bern

ARKANSAS
Mississippi River
Memphis
TENNESSEE
Chattanooga
Tennessee River
HOOD 1864
SHERMAN 1865
SCHOFIELD
1865
Wilmington
Fort Fisher
TERRY 1865

SOUTH CAROLINA
Columbia
Savannah River

MISSISSIPPI
Kennesaw Mtn
Atlanta
ALABAMA
SHERMAN 1864

Vicksburg
Montgomery
GEORGIA
Charleston
Fort Sumter
ATLANTIC OCEAN

Savannah

LOUISIANA
Mobile
Pensacola
Jacksonville
New Orleans
SHIP ISLAND
Gulf of Mexico
FLORIDA
St. Augustine

SCALE OF MILES
0   50   100   150   200

News of the fall of Atlanta sent the North into a frenzy of celebration. Not only had the Confederacy been deprived of its most vital arsenal and transportation hub, but the Union's resolve to continue the war had been rekindled. Sherman's victory virtually assured Lincoln's reelection.

Sherman decided to destroy Atlanta's arsenals and industrial areas. That way, he would not have to leave a large force in the city to defend these valuable properties against a Southern effort to recapture them. On November 15, 1864, Sherman left the burning city of Atlanta and began his march from Atlanta to the sea. Using the confiscation act of 1862 to justify his actions, Sherman left a path of burned or destroyed homes, plantations, and communities in his wake.

During the winter of 1865, Lee kept his army in Richmond, the Confederate capital. As the winter months progressed, the city became very somber. Its citizens seemed to be keeping a death watch, wondering which would expire first, the Confederate government or its army. General Lee could not attract

Sherman's March to the Sea

After conquering Atlanta in August 1864, General Sherman put into effect his understanding of what Lincoln meant by "total warfare." The entire South was the enemy, not just the Confederate army. "We are not fighting hostile armies, but a hostile people, and must make old and young, rich and poor, feel the hard hand of war," Sherman said.

Sherman proposed to General Grant a march across Georgia to Savannah, "smashing things to the sea." The purpose, he said, was to destroy the enemy's will to fight. On November 15, with Grant's permission, Sherman set out on his march. He left Atlanta in flames and headed east, destroying railroad lines and burning farms and plantations all the way to Savannah, while Georgian civilians stood by in horror.

One group of Georgians—the black slaves—welcomed Sherman's army. They thronged the roadsides and greeted the marching soldiers with roaring cheers. Thousands of them packed up their few belongings and fell in behind the Union soldiers.

General Beauregard urged Georgians to "arise for the defense of your native soil!" With most of Georgia's healthy men off fighting in Virginia and Tennessee, the only troops that could be mustered to stop Sherman were mostly old men and young boys. A band of four thousand of them gathered at Griswoldville to attack Sherman's army of seventy thousand. These brave but untrained men charged again and again, falling one after another to the Yankees' repeating rifles.

On December 13, Sherman reached Fort McAllister south of Savannah, the last major Confederate obstacle in his path to the sea. The fort was weakly defended, however, and the Union army occupied it after a fifteen-minute charge. In a month's time, Sherman's men had sliced the South in two, leaving a path of destruction sixty miles wide and three hundred miles long. Behind them, 317 miles of railroad track had been twisted around trees. The charred ruins of mills, factories, and farms filled the Georgia landscape. To his critics who questioned the necessity of such destruction, Sherman replied, "The more awful you can make war, the sooner it will be over.... War is hell, at best."

This engraving depicts Sherman's march to the sea. Sherman, mounted, left, surveys the destruction wrought by his troops as freed black slaves (right) attempt to follow the Union troops.

enough recruits to replace deserters. Many of the loyal Rebels who stayed on suffered from hunger, dysentery, and pneumonia. On March 25, 1865, in a desperate action, Lee sent his army on a surprise attack against the Union lines at Fort Stedman, outside Petersburg. When that attack was repelled, Lee knew that his army could no longer remain in Richmond.

On Sunday, March 26, Lee informed President Davis that Richmond and Petersburg were doomed. On April 2, Jefferson Davis and the members of his cabinet and other officers of the Confederate government abandoned their capital and headed for Danville, Virginia. To the dismay of the local citizens, they had the city's warehouses burned to keep their valuable contents from the enemy.

Grant's army quickly overwhelmed the Confederates at Five Forks, and the remnants of Lee's troops retreated farther to the west. On April 6, at Sayler's Creek, the Yankees overran the Rebels again. Six thousand Confederate soldiers were taken prisoner, including Richard Ewell and seven other generals.

General Grant spent the night of April 7 at Prince Edward Hotel in Farmville, where Lee had spent the previous night. There, he wrote a short message to Robert E. Lee:

> The results of the last week must convince you of the hopelessness of further resistance. I feel that is so, and regard it as my duty to shift from myself the responsibility of any further

Black refugees prepare to leave Richmond with their household belongings after the city falls to Union troops.

The ruins of an arsenal at Richmond. Confederates burned such arsenals rather than have them fall into Union hands.

effusion of blood, by asking of you the surrender of that portion of the Confederate States army known as the Army of Northern Virginia.

Lee was on the march the next morning, leading his army to Lynchburg when he received Grant's message. In response, he asked Grant to meet him between the two lines at 10:00 the next morning. That evening, Lee summoned his top commanders. Their situation could not have been more bleak. Union soldiers had just seized Appomattox Station, and with it, four trains loaded with food for Lee's army. All around them, the red campfires of the enemy glowed like the eyes of a pack of wolves, waiting to descend on its prey. Yet Lee's commanders voted not to surrender.

Early the next morning, April 9, the old II Corps of the Army of Northern Virginia, first commanded by Stonewall Jackson, then at Gettysburg by Richard Ewell, and finally in the Shenandoah Valley by Jubal Early, went into its final battle under a new commander, Gen. John Gordon. For three hours, the Confederates tried to hold out against an overwhelming Union advantage. Seeing this, Lee murmured to himself, "There is nothing left me but to go see General Grant, and I had rather die a thousand deaths."

Black Soldiers in Combat

When Abraham Lincoln first called for black soldiers to enlist in the Union army, they were expected to be used only for manual labor and not for combat. Although some blacks had fought bravely in the Revolutionary War, most white officers in the 1800s believed that they would make inferior soldiers.

It was not until 1864 that Frederick Douglass and other abolitionists persuaded Lincoln to allow black regiments to carry weapons. The first black regiment to enter into combat was the Fifty-fourth Massachusetts, under Col. Robert Gould Shaw. Shaw, like all commissioned officers of these black regiments, was white, since the army still forbade commissioning black officers.

Nevertheless, the soldiers of the Fifty-fourth led the Union charge on Fort Wagner, a Confederate earthwork defending Charleston Harbor on July 18, 1863. More than half of the regiment was killed or wounded in this one gruesome charge, including Colonel Shaw, who took a bullet in the heart. But the black soldiers gained the fort's main entrance, and their heroism was much publicized. It brought a change

Black soldiers stare fiercely at the camera.

in the public perception of black soldiers, and thereafter, black regiments were instrumental in many of the late Union campaigns, especially at Petersburg, Richmond, and on Sherman's march to the sea.

These black slaves stand ready to join the Union army.

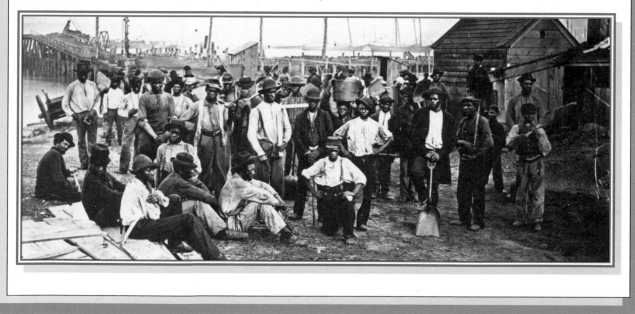

A horseman reached Grant with Lee's request to meet. Grant replied that he "would push forward to the front for the purpose of meeting you." He also made it clear that he had no intention of meeting with Lee for any purpose other than the surrender of his army.

When Lee received Grant's note, he rode toward Appomattox Court House, a small Virginia town. His aide rode ahead and arranged for a suitable meeting place. By remarkable coincidence, the house that was chosen, a two-story brick structure with a colonnade porch, belonged to Wilmer McLean. McLean had once owned a home near Manassas Junction, that had been used by General Beauregard as the Confederate headquarters during the First Battle of Bull Run. McLean was a loyal Southerner, but he had long since grown weary of the war in northern Virginia. He had moved to the little community of Appomattox Court House because "here the sound of battle will never reach us." But in its final moments, the war had reached McLean again.

The scene at the McLean home was a study in contrasts. Lee, white-bearded and tall, had put on his best uniform and wore his finest sword. Grant, slouched and red-whiskered, had a mud-spattered coat and no sword.

Grant offered Lee generous terms of surrender. Instead of taking all Lee's men prisoner, they would be paroled, with "all arms, ammunition, and supplies to be delivered as captured property." Then, Lee made one final request: "The cavalrymen and artillerymen own their own horses in our army. I would like to understand whether these men will be permitted to retain their horses."

The scene of Lee's surrender to Grant at the McLean home at Appomattox Court House.

At first, Grant refused, then he reconsidered. He would instruct the parole officers "to let all the men who claim to own a horse or mule take their animals home with them to work their little farms."

"This will have the best possible effect on the men," Lee said. Then the two gentlemen signed the document detailing their agreement. The war was over, at 3:00 P.M. on April 9, 1865, almost four years to the day after it had begun.

Soon, the Union camps were erupting in joy. George Meade, who had been so sick all week that he had scarcely left his bed, jumped on a horse and took off at a gallop, waving his hat and shouting, "It's all over, boys!" An officer who observed the surrender described the scene among the Yankee troops: "Men shouted until they could shout no longer; the air above us was for half an hour filled with caps, coats, blankets and knapsacks.... Huge, lumbering, bearded men embraced and kissed like schoolgirls, then danced and sang and shouted, standing on their heads and playing at leapfrog with each other."

On April 12, 1865, the scene was more somber as the men of the Army of Northern Virginia surrendered their weapons and regimental flags. As the Confederates came forward, marching through a double column of Yankee soldiers, Union general Joshua Chamberlain barked a command. Instantly, hundreds of Union muskets were raised in salute to their foes, the valiant soldiers of the Confederacy.

Then, the Confederate general John Gordon wheeled his horse in Chamberlain's direction. As the animal reared, General Gordon raised his sword high in the air and brought its tip swiftly down to his toes. He shouted a command, and the advancing Confederate army returned the salute. General Chamberlain recalled the moment:

> It was honor answering honor, and it was hard to say who was the more moved. Many of the grizzled veterans wept like women, and my own eyes were as blind as my voice was dumb. Not a sound of trumpet more, nor roll of drums; not a cheer, nor word, nor whisper of vain-glorying, nor motion of man standing again at the order, but an awed stillness rather, and breath-holding, as if it were the passing of the dead.

Confederate general John Gordon.

A Legacy of Bitterness

The outcome of the Civil War had altered the entire nation so drastically that it could not go back to the way it was. Slavery was dead in the United States and could never be revived. Although many Southerners refused to acknowledge it, clinging to the grand traditions and even passing them on to their children, the plantation system had to change. Southern landowners no longer had the power or the wealth to control the political direction of the nation.

The Union victory meant that the Northern vision would become the American vision. The nation became a modern, industrial, free enterprise economy. During the war, without Southern opposition, the Republican Congress had enacted an income tax system, funded a transcontinental railroad, and created a homestead policy. These all helped to establish a more powerful federal government.

In many ways, the Civil War transformed the nation from a weak confederation of states into the United States. Before this war, the federal government rarely touched the average citizen except through the post office. After the war, it became a vital player in people's lives by taxing them, drafting men into the army, creating a national currency and a national banking system, expanding the federal court system, and even establishing the first social welfare system—for freed slaves.

Until Abraham Lincoln became president, every U.S. president had been favored by the slaveholding residents of the Southern states. Southern domination of the Senate and the Supreme Court was even more conspicuous. After the Civil War, however, a full century passed before a resident of an ex-Confederate state became president. In half a century, only five of twenty-six Supreme Court justices were from the South, and none of the Speakers of the House of Representatives or presidents pro tem of the Senate were Southerners.

The spirit of reconciliation that President Lincoln had hoped for did not materialize. Instead, bitterness between Northerners and Southerners remained for many decades, and it was not long after the war that the bitterness began to surface.

On April 14, 1865, two days after the war ended, the president and Mrs. Lincoln decided to attend an evening of comedy at Ford's Theater, six blocks from the White House. As he and his wife entered the theater shortly before 8:30 P.M., Lincoln appeared more relaxed than at any time since he had become president. He also looked tired and far older than his fifty-six years.

A little after 10:00 P.M., a handsome but gloomy young actor named John Wilkes Booth walked through the theater lobby and up the stairs to the balcony. Booth, who had once served in the Virginia militia and was known for his fierce loyalty to the Southern cause, then slipped swiftly into the corridor behind the presidential box.

At 10:15, while the audience was roaring with laughter at the incidents on stage, the actor stepped into the presidential box, pulled a small derringer pistol from under his coat, and shot

After the Civil War, the South's entire infrastructure lay in ruins. Sherman's destructive march to the sea left many Southerners deeply embittered.

John Wilkes Booth assassinates President Abraham Lincoln. Booth's actions were inspired by the bitterness he felt over the outcome of the Civil War.

Abraham Lincoln in the back of the head. Then, Booth leapt down to the stage from the balcony, limped across the stage, made his way to the theater's rear exit, mounted a waiting horse, and vanished into the night.

Nine hours later, at 7:22 A.M. on April 15, 1865, Abraham Lincoln died. On April 26, John Wilkes Booth was tracked down and shot to death in a burning barn near Bowling Green, Virginia. On July 7, Lewis Paine, George Atzerodt, David Herold, and Mary Surratt were hanged for their role as accomplices in the assassination of President Lincoln and attempted assassinations of Vice President Andrew Johnson and Secretary of State William Henry Seward.

Hope for a generous and peaceful reconciliation with the South died with President Lincoln. Like the war that had torn the nation in two, the healing process would take longer than anyone expected. Radical Republicans, who still controlled Congress in 1865, had disagreed with Lincoln's gentle approach to the South. They wanted to make sure Southern slaveholders had learned a lesson. They offered no compensation to these slaveholders who had lost their slaves.

At the same time, Congress established a Committee on Reconstruction that recommended laws to rebuild the South the way radical Republicans wanted it rebuilt. They prohibited any former Confederate officer from holding public office. They required the former Confederate states to reapply for statehood with new constitutions. One condition for statehood was ratifying the Fourteenth Amendment, which gave blacks—and all men born or naturalized in the United States—all the rights of citizenship.

Many Southerners refused to accept the new social order that the North was dictating. Indeed, a large number of wealthy Southern families tried to maintain the same kind of plantation life-style they had had before the Civil War. They could not keep slaves, of course, but many of the freed slaves, with no money, education, or job training, had little choice but to go to work for their former masters as sharecroppers. A sharecropper worked the land owned by another and gave a portion of his crops to the landlord as rent.

The majority of white people in the United States still believed that they were superior to blacks. With the Southern economy in shreds and many former soldiers out of work, it was easy to blame free blacks and Republicans for all the South's problems. Mobs of white men decided to do something about it. They formed white supremacy groups, like the Ku Klux Klan, to terrorize blacks and their white sympathizers.

Gradually, Southern whites regained control of their cities and states. Blacks were free, but in most Southern states, many were not allowed to vote because they could not read and write or because they could not afford to pay the poll tax required to vote. The Civil War may have brought an end to slavery, but it did not eradicate racial injustice and prejudice in the United States. Today, that heritage remains.

After the Civil War, as veterans began telling their stories, a spirit of mutual respect among the former soldiers began to emerge. Remarkably, it was the men who had actually fought the war who took the first steps to start mending its wounds. In the mid-1870s, Union and Confederate veterans held joint reunions. They returned captured battle flags to survivors of the regiments that had lost them. They commemorated their fallen comrades. In 1875, at ceremonies in Massachusetts, Gen. William Francis Bartlett declared: "I am as proud of the men who charged so bravely with Pickett's division on our lines at Gettysburg, as I am of the men who so bravely met and repulsed them there."

Glossary

abolitionist a member of a movement that called for eradicating slavery in the United States and granting citizenship to freed slaves.

amputate to surgically remove all or part of an arm or leg.

arsenal a place for manufacturing or storing guns and ammunition.

artillery mounted guns, such as cannons; also, the troops that operate such guns.

battery a group of cannons or other artillery pieces.

blockade runner a small gunboat used by the Confederate navy to dodge Union ships that blocked Southern ports.

brigade a military unit smaller than a division and made up of several regiments.

brigadier general a general in command of a brigade.

canister a metal cylinder filled with shot that bursts and scatters when fired from a cannon.

cartridge a case for holding a single charge of gunpowder to fire a bullet from a gun.

casualty a soldier killed or wounded in battle.

cavalier a gentleman soldier, from the tradition of the French nobility.

cavalry troops trained to fight on horseback.

company the smallest military unit, usually about one hundred men.

Confederate of or related to the Confederate States of America, composed of the eleven Southern states that seceded from the United States.

confiscation the act of seizing property by official authority.

corps a large military unit made up of two or more divisions.

counterattack an attack made in response to another attack.

desert to leave military service and not return, in violation of one's duty.

division a military unit smaller than a corps but containing two or more brigades.

earthwork a construction formed mostly of earth for protection from enemy fire.

emancipate   to free from slavery.

enfranchise   to grant the right to own property or vote.

entrench   to strengthen a position by digging trenches around it.

fife   a small, high-pitched flute, used especially in early American military bands.

flank   one side of a military formation.

flotilla   a small fleet of boats or ships.

ford   to cross a river or stream by wading; also, the shallow part of a river or stream that can be used for crossing.

fortification   a wall built to defend a population against attack.

guardhouse   military jail.

inauguration   the ceremony of being sworn into office.

infantry   soldiers trained, armed, and equipped to fight on foot.

ironclad   a ship with an iron exterior. The ironclads used in the Civil War had wooden hulls and were covered with iron from the deck up.

junction   a place where roads, or railroads, meet.

limited war   a military strategy that aims to control, or limit, damage and casualties to the enemy.

magazine   a holder for cartridges to be fed into a gun automatically.

militia   the portion of a state's population that can legally be called to military service.

musket   a Civil War rifle that fired balls of lead instead of pointed bullets.

outflank   to advance around the enemy's flank.

picket   a soldier positioned to guard an army unit from surprise attack.

poll tax   a tax that one is required to pay before being allowed to vote; now illegal in the United States.

ratify   to officially approve something.

ration   a daily food allowance.

Rebel   a soldier fighting for the Confederacy.

rebel yell   a bloodcurdling scream uttered in unison by Rebel soldiers as they charged into battle.

reconnaissance   the collecting of military intelligence by scouting or spying on the enemy.

Reconstruction   the reorganization of the Confederate states for readmission to the Union following the Civil War.

recruit   to enlist new soldiers.

regiment   a military unit smaller than a brigade and made up of several companies.

repeating rifle   a rifle equipped with a magazine containing several cartridges so that it can be fired several times before reloading.

secede   to formally withdraw from an organization.

sharecropper   a farmer who lives and works on another person's land and pays the owner a share of the crop as rent.

shot   small lead pellets, often loaded inside canisters that were fired from a cannon.

shrapnel   a cone-shaped canister loaded with shot and a powder charge. After being launched, the shrapnel would explode and send shot flying in all directions.

siege   a military blockade of a city or fort to force it to surrender.

skirmisher   a soldier positioned in the very front of an advancing army unit.

states' rights   the rights of individual states to make their own laws on issues that do not affect national security, such as slavery or education, and to assume powers that the Constitution does not grant to the federal government or forbid to the states.

tourniquet   a bandage twisted tightly around an arm or leg to stop the bleeding from a wound.

Union   1) the whole nation of the United States; 2) the twenty-two states that did not secede from the United States at the beginning of the Civil War.

volley   a round of gunfire from a battery of guns.

Yankee   a resident of the northern United States; originally, a resident of New England.

For Further Reading

Roger Bruns, *Abraham Lincoln*. New York: Chelsea House Publishers, 1986.

David Donald, *Divided We Fought*. New York: Macmillan, 1961.

Trevor N. Dupuy, *The First Book of Civil War Naval Actions*. New York: Franklin Watts, 1961.

Neil Johnson, *The Battle of Gettysburg*. New York: Four Winds Press, 1989.

Robert Paul Jordan, *The Civil War*. Washington, D.C.: National Geographic Society, 1969.

Zachary Kent, *The Story of the Surrender at Appomattox Court House*. Chicago: Children's Press, 1987.

_____, *The Story of Sherman's March to the Sea*. Chicago: Children's Press, 1987.

R. Conrad Stein, *The Story of the* Monitor *and the* Merrimac. Chicago: Children's Press, 1983.

Martin Windrow, *The Civil War Rifleman*. New York: Franklin Watts, 1985.

Works Consulted

Henry Steele Commager, *The Blue and the Gray*. Indianapolis: Bobbs-Merrill, 1950.

R. Ernest Dupuy and Trevor N. Dupuy, *The Compact History of the Civil War*. New York: Hawthorn Books, 1960.

Shelby Foote, *The Civil War—A Narrative*. New York: Random House, 1963.

Lizzie Hardin, *The Private War of Lizzie Hardin*. Frankfort: The Kentucky Historical Society, 1963.

James McPherson, *Battle Cry of Freedom*. New York: Knopf, 1987.

_____, *Ordeal by Fire: The Civil War and Reconstruction*. New York: Knopf, 1982.

Milton Meltzer, ed., *Voices from the Civil War*. New York: Thomas Y. Crowell, 1989.

Reid Mitchell, *Civil War Soldiers*. New York: Viking, 1988.

Fletcher Pratt, *The Civil War*. Garden City, NY: Doubleday, 1955.

Geoffrey C. Ward, *The Civil War: An Illustrated History*. New York: Knopf, 1990.

Index

Photo Credits

Cover photo: Library of Congress

The Bettmann Archive, 6 (both), 9 (bottom), 12 (both), 13, 15, 19, 28 (bottom), 116, 126

Courtesy of the Connecticut Historical Society, 47 (top)

The Daughters of the Republic of Texas Library, 31

The Granger Collection, 95

Library of Congress, 7 (both), 34 (bottom), 36 (right), 37 (left), 38 (top), 42 (bottom), 43, 46, 48, 54, 55, 56, 61, 62 (top, bottom right), 63, 65, 66 (both), 67, 68, 71 (left), 72, 77, 78, 81, 83 (left), 85 (left), 87, 90 (right), 91, 93, 94, 95, 98, 101, 102, 103, 104, 107, 109 (right), 111, 112 (both), 115, 119, 121 (left), 122 (left), 127, 129 (top), 130, 134

Louis A. Warren Lincoln Library and Museum, 32

Francis Trevelyan Miller, ed., *Photographic History of the Civil War in Ten Volumes.* New York: The Review of Reviews Co., 1911, 83 (right)

National Archives, 9 (top), 10, 16, 18 (left, bottom), 21, 26, 27, 34 (top), 35, 36 (left), 37 (right), 38 (bottom left), 40, 41, 42 (top), 44, 45, 50, 52, 57, 58, 59, 60, 62 (bottom left), 71 (right), 74, 79, 80, 85 (right), 86 (both), 106, 120 (both), 121 (right), 122 (right), 124, 128, 129 (bottom), 131, 132, 133

National Portrait Gallery, Smithsonian Institution, 17, 18 (center), 25, 28 (top)

Prints Old & Rare, 47 (bottom left and right), 90

About the Author

Timothy Levi Biel was born and raised in eastern Montana. A graduate of Rocky Mountain College, he received a Ph.D. in literary studies from Washington State University. He is currently teaching in the communications department of the University of Texas at Arlington.

He is the author of numerous nonfiction books, many of which are part of the highly acclaimed Zoobooks series for young readers. In addition, he has written *The Black Death: World Disasters,* and several other books for Lucent Books.